An honest look

CW00731896

Cold Cups of Tea & Hiding in the Loo

Annie Willmot

CWR

For my granny, Jean Stevenson.
I learnt so much from you about what it
means to be a mum.
Our boys would have adored you.

Contents

Foreword

There are two types of people when it comes to children. There are those people who are pretty indifferent to kids until they have their own. Then there are those who just love kids. Annie is the latter. Long before she became a mum, she and her husband, Pete, were known as the amazing couple who semi-parented everyone else's kids!

The encouraging thing about parenthood is that no matter how experienced we are with children, when it comes to being a parent for the first time, each of us is a beginner. Nothing can prepare you for holding your own newborn for the first time, and the first smile; and nothing can prepare you for labour, sleep deprivation, and a baby who just will not stop crying. The power of Annie's writing is that she doesn't set herself up as an expert – despite being very qualified! On the contrary, she's like the rest of us, desperately trying to work out how to become a good parent, and never quite feeling up to the mark.

I first met Annie when she was in her early twenties living in London. I was a new mum in the throes of parenting. I had a three-year-old and a one-year-old (and went on to have two more babies after that). None of my children were sleepers. I was utterly exhausted and inclined to do ridiculous things, ranging from driving across London with my house keys on the car roof, to going out for the entire day leaving the front door wide open. Early parenthood is a very strange season of life.

I've always said, if someone set up a video camera in my house, no one would believe the madwoman I had become: running up and down the stairs in a frenzy, hair unwashed, milk all over my t-shirt, arms full of clothes, tripping over children and toys, forgetting where I was heading, one minute playing princess and the next minute shrieking 'STOP!' as a toddler pours a smoothie into my shoe, just for fun (all of this is real by the way).

Annie and Pete were quick to get stuck into our chaotic lives. Our children's meltdowns didn't seem to faze them. They were always willing to babysit or take them out and give us a break. I remember them taking our children out for milkshakes and a game of football one Saturday. After about an hour, they arrived home early to get more trousers for our son, who had managed to tip his entire chocolate milkshake all over himself. Annie had lovingly bought him a second drink, and then come back for some clean clothes. Fully imagining they were finished for the day, I said how grateful I was for the break. But Annie had no intention of bringing them back this early. With a clean set of clothes on, they headed back out for a game of football and a BBQ in the park with a group from church.

We didn't know at the time how precious this kind of supportive community was. It's not always easy to find. But time and again, Annie and Pete, before they even had children of their own, were blessing other families. They would have church kids over for the weekend to give their parents a break, and give respite to families who had children with special needs. Annie always had a stash of arts and crafts at home for when small people visited, while Pete was always found at church with about ten kids clambering on his shoulders.

Cold Cups of Tea & Hiding in the Loo pretty much summarises life with small children: never having time for yourself, and eventually needing to escape to the bathroom to find two minutes of peace and solitude amid the background noise of washing machines spinning, babies crying, electronic toys whirring and cartoons blaring out. The problem is that it's really hard to admit that sleeplessness, cold tea and screaming children are horrible. It's hard to admit that becoming a parent isn't everything you dreamed it would be; instead it comes with huge cost and self-sacrifice. At times, it's boring and at times, it's lonely. It's also absolutely incredible in many, many ways – but it's easy to talk about the joys of parenthood. It's not easy to admit the lows. And yet God is in the shadows and the unseen. His heart is with the humble, and with those who serve; His grace is sufficient for this season. *Cold Cups of Tea & Hiding in the Loo* wants to lead you to have a big honest conversation about all of it. The highs and lows and everything in between, and how to find God in the midst of it all.

Annie's book genuinely had me laughing out loud as I recognised so much of myself in her own experiences of parenthood. But it also offers so much wisdom about surviving the tough days. Community and friendship are a big feature of the book – something Annie lived and modelled long before she became a mum herself. It's impressive how she saw the need for all of us, whatever our stage of life, to be involved in parenting one another's children. We were never intended to take on this huge challenge of raising another human being in isolation.

While Annie utterly identifies with all the stress of raising young children, she also offers wisdom and ideas for staying connected to God and a wider community throughout these key years.

With rising awareness of mental health, and the impact of postnatal depression among mums, Annie's book is a timely and helpful guide for all parents as they enter this amazing new season. It's a perfect blend of humour, tears, practical advice and spiritual wisdom. I wish Annie and Pete were still living around the corner from us. I know we'd have all been as involved in our children's lives as we were in our London days. I'm so glad she's given us all this honest glimpse into her own experience of motherhood. Her book challenges us to start talking with the same level of vulnerability and honesty, and encourages us to carry one another's burdens (and children!) as we journey together through parenthood.

Becky Drake

Introduction

A few months after I'd had my first baby, I was chatting with a friend who was also a new mum. Sitting together in my messy living room, soothing our grumpy babies and drinking our cooling cups of tea, I asked her, 'How are you finding it?' She paused before replying, 'Can I be honest? I'm not enjoying it.'

She was struggling.

She loved her child but was finding being a mum hard and wondered whether she was allowed to feel this way. When she had tried to talk to her health visitor, rather than receive support or understanding, she'd received unhelpful criticism that made her feel judged. She'd been made to feel that she should be loving every moment – or at least acting like it.

My friend's willingness to be vulnerable and to share how she was feeling kick-started something in me. I wanted to figure out how to create space for more open, honest and vulnerable conversations. I wanted other parents to know that they didn't have to pretend that everything was fine.

So, I began to write honestly about my experience of motherhood.

All of it.

The good days.

The bad days.

The incredibleness of growing a human life, but also

the harsh reality of feeling sick all day, every day. Having a brilliant conversation with your toddler about God one moment, then seeing them bite another kid in the next.

Whether your child grew inside your body or whether you chose to adopt them into your family, becoming a mother is an incredible, wonderful thing. But that doesn't mean it isn't hard. It doesn't mean that you have to pretend that you are enjoying every single moment, or that you're OK *all* the time.

Pregnancy nausea and sickness, sleepless nights, being covered in baby poo, vomit and wee, struggling to settle a screaming baby or arguing with your partner because you're too tired to think straight are all difficult challenges individually, let alone when they are combined. No parent needs the added stress of having to pretend that everything is under control all of the time.

Parenting isn't easy, which is why having support is vital. Hopefully, most of us have opportunities to develop relationships – with our family, with friends, and with our community – so that we are not alone. But we also have a relational God. If we choose to invite Him, He dwells right in the midst of real life with us. He can be central to each of our journeys as we explore what parenthood, family and community look like for our own lives. And the beautiful thing is that our relational God created family. His Son, Jesus, was born right into family life.

Family relationships are sometimes messy and dysfunctional. Mary had travelled roughly 80 miles, either on foot or on a donkey, before giving birth to God's Son in a stable. I can't quite imagine a more messy start!

The Bible is full of stories of families who haven't

quite got it together. Take Jacob, for example, whose favouritism towards one son angered the other 11 so much they plotted to kill him (Gen. 37:17–20). Then there's King Saul who became estranged from his son, Jonathan, when his son chose to protect his best friend (1 Sam. 20:30–34). Even Mary and Joseph once left a young Jesus behind in Jerusalem and had to go back and get Him (Luke 2:43–48)!

All families are different. They're messy in their own beautiful, and not so beautiful, ways. Families have different ideas about what being a family means, what values to hold on to, and how to connect with God at home. When families talk and share these ideas, they connect. The conversations had in the car dashing from one place to another; when we stop tidying to listen to what's bothering our kids; when we're making big decisions and, as a family, we talk and pray about them – these are all opportunies to connect. There's no magic formula for how to be a family. We're each on our own journey. However, when we connect with each other as mothers, fathers, friends and family, we can bring so much joy and richness to each other's lives.

When we are prepared to be vulnerable, we can learn from and encourage each other in hard times, as well as celebrate joyful times together. When we choose vulnerability, connection can happen in the messiness of everyday life.

So if you are looking for a book on how to have a tidy house, raise well-mannered kids, fit in all the activities that come with family life and be connected with God, I'm afraid that you're going to be disappointed. Besides, is all of that even possible?

This book is about honesty and vulnerability. It is a book written by a parent trying to figure out how to do faith during this phase of life. There will be opportunities to pause and reflect and to spend time with God throughout – but no pressure to do that every day. This is a book you can pick up and put down whenever you manage to find time. My hope is that this book will encourage you in your faith during this early parenting phase, and lead you into stronger, deeper and more open connection with your family, friends, children and God.

One day we hope to adopt, but right now my family is my husband, our two sons and me. This book is written from that perspective, but also my experiences from working with children and families as well as stories from other parents and grandparents. It's an ongoing learning process, and the ideas and tips are not shared as an expert but as someone who has relished learning from others and who hopes that they might be helpful to others.

If you are single, married, or somewhere in between, with children, then this book is for you. (Many of the challenges we face in parenthood aren't limited to a specific age or stage.) I hope that this book will help you to breathe a sigh of relief and feel more confident to be honest and vulnerable and to laugh at how truly ridiculous parenthood can feel sometimes – because, let's be honest, it can!

Becoming 'mum' and 'dad'

Becoming a mum is a huge life shift. It's an all-consuming role. It doesn't fit neatly into a box, no matter how much we might try to cram it in. Instead, it splays out into every area of our life.

When we start to be defined as a 'mum', we can feel as if we have lost who we were, or who we thought we might have been becoming. Suddenly the goals we were aiming for, or the things we hoped we might achieve, seem distant. That's not to say we don't feel overwhelmingly grateful to receive the title of 'mum', it just takes some adjusting when it comes to our identity.

I am a writer, preacher, pastor, coordinator, blogger, young people's coach, daughter, wife, friend and sister. But, primarily, in this phase of my life, 'mum' (or 'Annie' when my eldest is being particularly cheeky) is the title that I hear the most. It's a role that I will now always carry. Even if my kids are asleep, or when they leave home one day, I'm still mum.

I am married to Pete who is a worship pastor and we have two boys, Big brother and Little brother (obviously, these are not their real names but, for as long as possible, we are trying to give them some anonymity). At the moment I spend a lot of my time chasing a toddler with a baby attached to me, finishing half-started craft activities, half-starting my own activities and desperately trying to keep up with the incredible amount of laundry produced by two small people (and a husband).

Pete and I knew, before we started our family, that we wanted to be really intentional about raising emotionally healthy kids who were confident talking openly about how they were feeling. But first we needed to make sure that we were honest and vulnerable with each other as a couple. We certainly don't get this right all the time. In fact, we fail pretty epically a lot of the time. But we are committed to being sincere and real in our marriage. In fact, much of this book comes from learning to be honest in other relationships as well as in my role as a parent.

Pete will also be sharing his own experiences and reflections about parenthood throughout this book. We're a team, and his voice and his point of view are so important in our family – we learn so much from one another when we share our own perspectives. He helps me to consider things I hadn't thought about and even (sometimes) to think differently.

Pete says...

I'm in the phase of being known as 'dad', 'daddy', 'dadu' (or sometimes even 'mama' — kids are the best, right?!) and I find such a joy in being a father. I love our boys to bits, in the good times and the bad times. When it comes to honest conversations, I would say it's taken me a long time to learn to be vulnerable and open. Like most guys (I assume), candid conversations don't tend to come naturally to me. However, since Annie and I decided to be more intentional about improving our communication, I've found a greater confidence in sharing things. Sure, there are times when it doesn't go so well, and we're still learning how to lovingly communicate. But as we keep going, those conversations start to come more naturally, and our relationship with each other deepens, hopefully modelling to our kids how to have an honest conversation with integrity and compassion.

There's no one right way to do parenthood. Or to do faith as a family. People have plenty of theories and ideas but ultimately it's going to look slightly different for everyone. Even how we became parents differs.

For some of us it's through birth, for others it's through adoption or fostering. Some of us are parents to step-children or have taken on parenting roles for children we're not related to. Some of us are parents who have lost our babies or children. However, *all* of us are unconditionally loved children of God – so, whatever way we become parents, let's take comfort in remembering who's parenting us:

> 'See what great love the Father has lavished on us, that we should be called children of God! And that is what we are!' 1 John 3:1

Parenthood carries many similar challenges but its expression is diverse. We all want to find ways to connect with our kids but how we do that will differ. Given how different our families are, it makes sense that there are different ways to parent. Yet somehow we feel there is an expectation on us to do it 'well', to do it a certain way – or to expect judgment however we choose to parent. Let's discover what works best for our own families, for our loved ones and have confidence to parent differently.

10

Honest confessions

I am deeply passionate about promoting honest conversations about the highs and lows of parenting, and what it's like to do faith as a parent – no judgment, just sharing experiences.

So, in the interest of honesty and vulnerability, here are ten things I have thought or done since I became a mum.

1. When my babies started sleeping through the night, it wasn't the cuddles or feeding I missed, it was getting to watch boxsets. It's quite hard to catch up on a series without those extra hours of night viewing.

2. Some days I struggle to think of 'enriching' activities for my kids – or I'm just exhausted – so they watch more TV than I might like to admit.

3. Before children, there were things I said I wouldn't do as a parent that I have since done, such as having one or both kids in bed with us.

4. Feeling incredibly lonely while surrounded by people, I have often wished that someone would just make eye contact with me at a toddler group.

5   Sometimes I go to the toilet just to try to get 30 seconds on my own.

6   I gave my baby a bottle of formula every now and then but told the health visitor that he was 'exclusively breastfed' because I couldn't face that conversation.

7   On multiple occasions, I have fished clothes out of the laundry basket to wear as I cannot keep up with the amount of washing.

8   I have counted the minutes on the clock until Pete came home from work so I could hand him a crying baby and stop playing the same game over and over again.

9   I have been jealous of Pete as he left for work.

10   I have hidden (and got rid of) toys and books that I just cannot face reading or playing with *again*.

These things don't mean that I am not doing a good job or that I don't love my kids dearly. But there have been many times when I felt that I couldn't honestly say something for fear that someone might think exactly that. What about you? What would you honestly say if you knew no one would judge you or doubt your abilities as a parent?

The pressure to be perfect

Before Big brother arrived, I thought I had it all sussed. Once I started maternity leave, I was going to finally have a completely clean and tidy house. I would regularly catch up with friends, do lots of writing, and maybe even take up some new hobbies – after all, babies do quick feeds and then sleep, right?

I had huge, and totally unrealistic, expectations. What really happened was that Pete would come home from work and I'd still be sat in the same chair, feeding the baby *again* and wondering what on earth I'd actually achieved that day.

The reality didn't seem to sink in though because when it came to baby number two, I still had massively high expectations for myself. I remember one occasion when I had my evening all planned out. Pete was at work. The boys would go to bed on time. I'd tidy the kitchen, put away the many mounds of washing, make myself a cup of tea and then sit down for an evening of work.

You may have guessed already that I fell at the first hurdle. Big brother went down very quickly (albeit in his 'floor bed' as he refused to sleep in his actual bed), Little brother, however, took *all* evening to settle. By the time he was down, I was knackered and desperate to sleep rather than do any of the others things I *needed* to do. Trying to achieve my perfect parent wish list wasn't just hard, it was impossible. The problem with trying to be a 'perfect mum' wasn't simply that I wanted to achieve too much, it was that I wanted to give 100% of my energy to every task and expectation I set myself.

When I was working from home, I was distracted by all the things that needed doing like the food shopping, or laundry. When I was playing with the kids, I was thinking about the cleaning I'd like to get done, what we should have for tea, or checking emails and planning what I needed to do once they'd gone to bed. My to-do list was never-ending and it was always weighing on my mind. It felt like trying to juggle 100 balls all at once. Even in real life, the most anyone has every managed to juggle is 11 balls. I checked!

I might have looked like I was doing well but I was struggling. And when I say struggling, I mean I was scrambling around on the floor trying to find the balls I'd dropped while all the others continued to fall on top of me. No one seemed to notice though. In fact, sometimes, they even commented on how well I seemed to be juggling everything. I felt like if I told them about my juggling inability they might laugh. I was sure everyone else had it sussed.

When I tried to be my idea of a perfect mum, I didn't feel fully present in any part of my life. I was exhausted – and I felt guilty *all the time*. Something had to change.

While trying to figure out where these expectations came from, I initially put the blame on Pete. But he told me that he didn't expect those things at all! He was happy to come home to a messy house if it meant that I'd spent quality time with the boys that day. I was the one setting ridiculously high standards for myself based on what I felt I should be doing, what I'd seen others do, and how my parents raised me. Wherever expectations come from, I do believe that we all have the power to change our priorities and this was something I wanted to do.

First I decided to write a list of what was expected of a perfect mother so I knew what I was dealing with. This is what I came up with:

- Get enough sleep and look after your body.
- Look after everyone else's health.
- Keep track of the whole family calendar.
- Make meal-plans and ensure everyone eats healthily.
- Buy everyone's clothes.
- Know where *everything* is for *everyone*.
- Go to parents' evenings and kid-related meetings.
- Do nursery drop-offs and get to work on time remembering your notebook, laptop etc.
- Focus 100% on your kids as 'they're only young once' but also progress in your career.
- Get all the laundry done and put away.
- Make costumes for fancy-dress days.
- Keep the house tidy and clean.
- Fix things when they break.
- Be thrifty and help save money but also spoil your children and family.

- Do Pinterest-worthy educational activities with your children.
- Teach your kids to use the potty, in fact teach them *all* life skills.
- Help your kids connect with God.
- Stay connected with God yourself.
- Date your husband and invest in your marriage.
- Enjoy your kids, after all, 'they're only young once...'.

I could go on...

Once I started to write my list, I realised how ridiculous it was. Previously I'd wondered, *Perhaps I'm just not very good at this,* or, *Maybe I just don't manage to do as much as other people.* But when I looked at the list, there was no denying that even the most energetic super-mum might find it hard to put 100% into all the things I thought I needed to do.

Sometimes reflecting where our expectations come from, maybe by writing them down or chatting to a partner or friend about them, is helpful. For me, writing them down meant I could move them from the voice in my head to a list I could look at objectively.

Whenever I'm struggling or feeling overwhelmed, I know the first thing I need to do is get my focus back on God. (In practice, I don't always remember this but when I do it changes my perspective immediately!)

When I read about how God tells us not to worry about tomorrow, I'm encouraged to focus on what is happening right now.

'Give your entire attention to what God is doing right now, and don't get worked up about what may or may not happen tomorrow. God will help you deal with whatever hard things come up when the time comes.' Matthew 6:34 (*The Message*)

For me, this was the biggest thing that needed to change: to put to one side all the thoughts of the future and striving for this ideal 'perfect mum' I'd created; and focus instead on what was happening right in front of me – choosing to live in the present.

I started to ask myself questions like: *Is it more important that I hold my kids and comfort them for as long as they need or that my washing is put away? Does it matter if we're a few minutes late for nursery because I stopped to play 'swords' with Big brother, or because we spent that little bit longer chatting over breakfast? Is it OK that some moving boxes aren't unpacked yet because we've chosen to spend more time resting and enjoying our new space?*

On paper, the answers seem obvious but I needed to re-learn those answers. I needed to remind myself to stop, to be present, to focus on God and my family, and to be in the moment.

Sometimes I write down the thing that's distracting me from being present, so I can come back to it later. Or admit to myself that spending quality time with my kid now means that I won't finish the job I just started – and being OK with that.

I remember a friend telling me about how she used to

hurry her daughter along when they walked places. Then one day she decided instead to join her little girl in sniffing the flowers and pottering along, taking everything in. They didn't need to be anywhere in a hurry. Rushing had become a habit, but when she stopped to be present, she found she was able to share more moments of joy with her daughter.

When everything feels overwhelming, I love to find a moment to sit and look out into our garden at the birds. It's one place where I will always feel really present and full of wonder at the beauty of God's creation. It's good to find a place where you can choose to be 100% present, even if only for a moment.

As we go through different seasons of parenthood, our priorities will change. My constant priorities are to connect with God, help my kids to connect with God, to develop my relationship with God and help my kids find their own relationship with Him. Everything else comes and goes.

Some seasons, I have new priorities and expectations so I put down some existing ones and pick up these new ones; like accepting that more meals will be coming from the freezer while I focus on the new job I've just started, or choosing not to serve on the welcome team at church for a while because my kid needs me with them during the start of the service. It's helpful to reflect on what's important for you in your current season – the juggling balls don't all need to be in the air at once.

Choosing not to give everything 100% can be a challenge, but letting go and ditching the mum-guilt can be so incredibly freeing. Here are some things I've done to try to make life that little bit easier.

Crafts

Some people are really great at crafty projects for kids, some aren't. If buying a craft kit means spending more quality time with our kids and not feeling stressed about gathering all the bits and pieces needed – then let's do it!

Cooking

Preparing healthy meals for our kids is important but sometimes, at the end of the day, it's hard to find the energy. I often used to feel guilty serving up 'snacky tea', which is basically whatever I can find in the cupboards when I haven't managed to cook or shop, and now it's Big brother's favourite meal. We've literally had tears because I cooked him a meal and all he wanted was 'snacky tea'.

Cleaning

I find the mess created by a baby, toddler and husband quite stressful, and when I went back to work I couldn't figure out how to keep on top of it all. Sometimes I have to try to ignore it until a day when either Pete or I can look after the kids for a couple of hours, while the other one blitzes the house. I've also had to accept that the only way for me to have a perfectly tidy house would be to move Pete and the boys out, and I think I love them just about enough to live with the mess.

Laundry

If I could afford to pay someone to put all my laundry away I would. Once, for an hour, I had an empty wash basket. It might actually have been one of my biggest accomplishments to date. In a house where washing didn't dry very quickly I found I was really struggling to get through all of our laundry, so I saved up to buy a heated airer and it is undoubtedly one of my most-loved possessions.

It might sound dramatic but allowing myself to cut corners and choosing not to feel guilty has transformed my experience of motherhood. We really do have the power to lower our expectations for ourselves and to ditch the mum-guilt. It's not necessarily a quick and easy process but it's one that is so worthwhile for our mental and physical health because constantly trying to achieve an impossible list of expectations is, quite frankly, exhausting.

We can be so focused on our own high expectations, keeping all the juggling balls in the air, that we might not notice when others are struggling. As well as taking practical steps ourselves, the more we talk about the challenge of parenting with others the more we can help shatter the illusion that we've got it all under control.

Pete says...

The typical stereotype of a father-figure is that he is the main provider, focused on his own career, and the occasional 'babysitter' when mum manages a night out. Some people express mild surprise when a dad is able to competently parent his kids when out and about alone with them. Does it need to be like that? Why can't the mother be the breadwinner or the father take shared parental leave? I admire fathers who decide not to pursue an overly demanding promotion or put systems in place at work so that they can be more present as a father. The more we talk about what really matters as parents, the more I've found it's helped me to remove the pressure to conform to social norms.

At school I was a bit of a geek: one of those weird people that actually liked writing essays. I was desperate for people to like me, with an unhealthy compulsion towards perfectionism and a 'need' to achieve 100%.

Becoming a mother has drawn out that same teenage predicament. It looks a little different but the insecurity is still there. Does my child like me? Am I doing it 'right'? Am I good enough?

As someone who loves exams, it baffles me that there isn't some test, some qualification needed in order to be a parent. But then maybe that's the point. You can read a million books, which talk about 'the average child', the 'average' weight, sleep time, wake time… But your child doesn't seem to fit 'the average'.

Slowly, slowly, slowly, I'm learning to put down the baby books and learning to trust. Trust myself. Trust my baby. I'm learning that getting it 'right' means simply to give love. He may have cried all day; I may have no idea why, and all the books and apps in the world can't explain it but to continue to love is good enough and right enough.

I may have needed a time out. A five minute break. I may have shoved him at my husband before I lost my mind. And my patience. But that isn't failure. That's sometimes what is needed to refill my tank to love again. And again. And again.

My mothering skills are not graded (thankfully!). But if I can get to the end of the day knowing that I loved my boy and gave him all I had, well then, A* it is. **Sarah**

THINKING HONESTLY

What are your priorities in your current season?

What roles might you need to put down to focus on your priorities?

Of all the things you feel you need to achieve, what brings you most joy?

I have absolutely no idea what I'm doing

I had all these visions of transitioning seamlessly into my new role as a mother: responding to my son's gentle cries, settling him into his basket for the night, and just generally glowing as I went about my days, drinking hot cups of tea and enjoying his peaceful gurgling.

In reality, it was a little bit less smooth than that. And when I say 'less smooth', I mean rather than the gentle cruise I had perhaps pictured it was a bit more like trying to cycle down a cobbled street while wearing flip-flops and trying to carry a very full bag of shopping.

When Big brother was born some friends gave us a book called *Zagazoo*[1]. When I first read it, I thought it was just a fun little story for kids. However, re-reading it recently, I now think it is one of the most accurate representations of parenthood.

A couple receive a package. Inside is a baby called Zagazoo. He's not without faults but they think he's pretty great. However, they wake up one morning to find that he's turned into a noisy baby bird of prey. They don't know what to do. Then suddenly, he's a clumsy elephant who causes chaos. They don't know how they'll manage. Then he turns into a filthy warthog, then a fiery dragon, then a shrieking bat, back to the warthog, then the elephant again, then back to the dragon... They can't keep up! Then one day he changed into an odd shaggy animal. He'd become a teenager. They questioned what they should do, and they wondered what on earth would happen to them. All of a sudden he became a well-rounded adult.

I had no idea that parenthood really could be like that. Just when you think you've sussed one thing, there's a new challenge thrown at you. One day a solution works, the next it doesn't. And each day you try your hardest to raise your kids the best you can, hoping that one day, when they're all grown up, you'll look back and know you did a good job.

Parenting is a bit like parachute jumping daily. Some days you find your parachute worked and you make a nice soft landing. Other days you find it didn't deploy correctly and you end up in a crumpled heap on the bathroom floor wondering what on earth went wrong.

I remember walking out of the hospital with our new baby. As I tentatively walked across the carpark, I wondered, *Why on earth have they let us take him?! We have no idea what we're doing!*

I've lost count of the number of times when I have looked at Pete and said, 'I don't know what to do,' or 'I have no idea what's wrong' – usually while holding a completely inconsolable child or having a furious toddler in the background.

I always used to be someone who struggled with the unknown. I'd do everything I could to figure out why something was happening. I wanted to know the correct answer. I needed to be in control. It's not always possible to do that with parenting. I have so many unanswered questions every day:

- Why are they sick?
- Why are they crying?
- What is my kid trying to say?
- Will not being consistent make it harder for us in the long run?
- Is he actually scared or does he just not want to go to bed?
- Would it have been better if I'd chosen a different nursery/school for him?
- Did I actually brush my teeth today?

Sometimes the weight of unanswerable questions can be paralysing, preventing me from confidently moving forward for fear of not having the right answer.

Before becoming a parent, I'd already been learning to put my trust in God daily and give Him my fears and unanswered questions. As parenthood added new questions I knew I couldn't answer, I would chat to God. 'God, I don't know what I am doing.' 'God, why is my baby behaving like that?' 'God, please help me.'

That didn't mean that I suddenly knew what I was doing, but I did move into a place of being OK with not knowing what I was doing. I knew that God did know all the answers and He was right by my side listening to me as I chatted to Him.

The reality is that we will never know *all* the answers but hopefully we can begin to think, 'I don't know everything and I'm OK with that.' We may still have days when we're overwhelmed and struggle with the unknown but, by taking our worries to God, we can learn to feel at peace in difficult times.

I used to work coaching unemployed young people and we taught them that they always have a choice. We would watch a video clip where some young people were in tricky situations, often feeling powerless in their circumstances, but they always had a choice.

The same is true in parenthood. It can be easy to take on a victim mentality, thinking there's nothing we can do, or that we have no power in a situation but we *always* have a choice. I can choose how to respond to my kid. I can choose my own behaviour. I can also choose to feel OK with not knowing how to respond.

On the messiest days of parenthood, I've definitely felt like a victim. Those days where everyone is sick, when there have been multiple tantrums, or it feels like everything has gone wrong. But actually I'm *choosing* to feel like a victim. I may not be able to make everyone healthy instantly, figure out what I did to upset my toddler or resolve the day's problems but I can choose how I'm going to respond. I'm not powerless.

That may sound easier said than done but when I started telling myself that I had a choice, it really did shift my attitude and how I reacted to situations. My circumstances might not have changed, the day might still have been pretty rubbish, but I knew I could choose how I was going to feel and behave in the midst of that rubbish-ness!

I will admit that I am quite stubborn, so some days I will

go through this thought process but still choose to feel like a victim, or choose to be cross or sad because I need to feel that before I move on. I'm not proud of feeling this way but this is me being honest. It's taken practice, and a whole lot of prayer, to totally shift my mindset and feel more powerful in all my choices. Friends now comment on my laid-back-ness and how chilled I am about things, which is not how people described me when I was growing up!

I often quote my mum, in my head, who told me, 'It's all guess work!' I found that so helpful, particularly in the newborn 'what do they want?!' phase.

I think there's a misconception that, as a mother, you'll just 'know' which cry means what, and have the instincts to know what they need. That skill develops but I also think a lot of the time it really is just guess work! I know I need to hold on to this concept even as my kids get older as we meet new challenges. **Jos**

Feeling like you don't know what you're doing is hard, but feeling like you *do* know what you're doing one minute and then having absolutely no idea the next might be even harder!

I wonder if, rather than knowing what we're doing *all* the time, it's more about how we can find constants in the unknown and the ups and downs. These constants might differ from person to person, but here are a few suggestions to get us thinking.

Connect with God

God is constant in the unknown. He is unchanging. He knows *all* of the answers (even if He doesn't always reveal them to us!) and He knows us and our children intimately. When we shift our focus on to Him, then the unknown seems to shrink in comparison. When I feel overwhelmed, it's almost like there's so much in my head that I can't find space to focus on God, so I often have to visualise handing over those unanswered questions and creating space for God.

I try to think intentionally about how I might connect with God before I have one of those full-on parenting days where I realise I didn't connect with Him at all. Paul's beautiful prayer for fellow believers in Ephesus is one I come back to again and again.

'I pray that out of his glorious riches he may strengthen you with power through his Spirit in your inner being, so that Christ may dwell in your hearts through faith. And I pray that you, being rooted and established in love, may have power, together with all the Lord's holy people, to grasp how wide and long and high and deep is the love of Christ, and to know this love that surpasses knowledge – that you may be filled to the measure of all the fullness of God. Now to him who is able to do immeasurably more than all we ask or imagine, according to his power that is at work within us, to him be glory in the church and in Christ Jesus throughout all generations, for ever and ever! Amen.' Ephesians 3:16–21

When I stop for a moment and read that passage, I remind myself of how incredibly powerful God is and that His power is at work within me. I don't know all the answers but I know that God is so much bigger. Even His love is like an unanswered question, which I will never fully understand. And that's OK!

Pete says...

Like many guys, finding solutions and fixing things is what I think I do best. Add a baby into the mix who can't communicate and suddenly all those solutions and simple fixes are gone. You feel out of your depth; you can't figure out the answers or find an easy fix. I find myself making up parenting as I go along. Part of my role at work is to isolate problems, especially with technology, and to methodically figure out where the fault lies. With our kids, I've found, this is not so easy! Sure, chances are that if they're crying at 4am and have been for the last seven hours, then they're feeling tired. That's a given, right? However, even though they're tired, there's so often something deeper bothering them, stopping them from achieving that sleep they want. We go through the basics (fed, clean and dry, comfortable, well in themselves), until, all of a sudden, they decide they're done crying and they go to sleep, and we can't figure out how we actually solved the problem. The toughest thing for me is remembering to stay calm, to chat to God in those moments and be real

> with Him. 'God, I'm struggling now and we all need
> some sleep... please help...' is absolutely OK to pray
> in those moments, and I've often experienced God
> saying back to me, 'Trust me, I'm here.'

Find friends who don't know either

A friend and I often message each other via text. Our conversations generally begin by one of us texting, 'I have no idea what to do about...' and the other replying, 'I didn't either. Here's what I tried...' Sharing ideas is helpful but the fact that we stand together in that unknown place, with total empathy and absolutely no judgment, is deeply reassuring.

If you're finding parenting hard, then ask a trusted friend to check in with you. Why not ask them to keep you accountable in choosing to be OK with not knowing everything.

Remember the moments when you knew you were doing a good job

When you're feeling like you don't know what you're doing, it can be easy to spiral into a place of feeling like you *never* know what you're doing or even doing a good job. In those moments, it's useful to remind yourself of times when your children thought you were the best mum or dad in the world. Those times when they came over to you and kissed your knee for absolutely no reason. Or when you did something and they said, 'Thanks mum' unprompted and really meant it.

Just recently Big brother told me he was proud of me for no particular reason. That phrase and his sweet little smile carried me through a very tearful week when both boys were poorly and I wasn't able to figure out how to fix things for them.

It's OK *not* to know what you're doing

Sometimes it seems like everyone else knows what they're doing. They don't. Well, enough parents have honestly admitted to me that they don't, to assume that the rest probably don't either.

I have found that one of the most powerful things I can teach my kids is that it's OK not to know what you're doing. As someone who has struggled with that, I want my kids to be comfortable with not knowing *all* the answers.

So when Big brother asks me a question, to which I don't know the answer, I confidently reply, 'I don't know. What do you think?' Sometimes we discuss the possible answers together, sometimes he replies, 'I don't know either', and sometimes we chat to God about what the answer might be. Whatever conversation follows, I know that he's also learning that it's OK not to know all the answers and I love that we're on that journey together.

THINKING HONESTLY

Are there verses that help you to know God's peace and presence in spite of feeling like you're completely overwhelmed by everything else?

Could you put those verses up somewhere or put one as your phone or computer background?

Would putting on worship music or watching worship videos help you to know God's peace and presence?

Can you start getting into the practice, maybe by writing them down, of handing over to God your unanswered questions?

[1]Quentin Blake, *Zagazoo* (London: Red Fox, 2000)

The advice begins

Once you tell people you're pregnant, or that you're adopting, you discover that everyone has advice to share.

'Be sure to get lots of rest before the baby comes.'

'Eat healthily and keep active.'

'I had a really traumatic labour. Take all the drugs they offer you.'

'I had a really easy labour in the birthing pool. You don't need to take any drugs.'

'I recommend you get this type of pushchair/car seat [insert other baby paraphernalia here].'

I found it totally overwhelming. I was still getting used to the idea of being pregnant and the prospect of potentially having to push a baby out of my body. (I don't think that one really sunk in fully until labour actually started.) I wasn't ready for how much other people would suddenly want to be involved. I certainly wasn't ready for the fact that advice would come even when I hadn't asked for it, and I made it clear that, for now, I was happy not to have any advice.

Sometimes, I want advice; sometimes I don't, preferring to figure it out on my own. The funny thing with advice is that when you don't want it, there seems to be plenty but when you do, it's hard to find. Then you end up down the rabbit hole that is the internet, reading masses of conflicting opinions and feeling none the wiser by the time you emerge. Or at least that's what I do anyway.

When the advice began, it surprised me that so much of it was completely contradictory. One person would tell me something and then another would give me the opposite piece of advice. Both would swear that their counsel was the best. What I found reassuring was that, despite their conflicting advice, both ladies had managed to get through pregnancy and their babies seemed to be doing OK.

The stream of advice doesn't stop once you've had your baby. It carries on. When your kid starts teething, or they're not sleeping, when they start nursery, then school, when they hit the 'tween' years... I'm pretty sure that for whatever aspect of parenthood you're going through, there'll be someone ready to give you advice (whether you want it or not!).

So, if it's unavoidable, how do we handle it? (I realise the irony of me now sharing advice with you! But everything I share in this book is for you to take or leave as you wish.) Here are some of the things I've learnt, and questions I've asked, when it comes to advice.

We can choose to do parenthood however we like!

One of the biggest revelations in parenting was realising that there isn't necessarily one right way to do things. It's down to me and Pete to choose how we want to raise our kids. If we want to have some daily fixed routines, but also be flexible about feeding them to sleep, then we can do just that. If we have some plan of when we will start weaning, but use our own method of mixing baby-led weaning and spoon feeding, then that's what we'll do. Just because someone else had 'success' doing one method doesn't mean that we have to do the same.

I have to keep reminding myself that I know my kids. I'm their mum and no one has parented *my* children before. There are pros and cons for every recommended method but, ultimately, Pete and I get to do this parenthood thing how we want to. The more this sunk in, the more I was able to gain confidence in myself and not feel overwhelmed by all the advice. I began to feel able to smile, nod and thank someone for their opinion while also thinking, *That advice isn't for me.*

Why are they giving me advice?

When someone is giving me advice that I didn't ask for, I try to understand where they're coming from. (Well, not so much in the moment, perhaps more on reflection afterwards.) I ask myself:

- Is this something they found hard, and so they want to talk about what they had achieved?
- Do they genuinely want to help?
- Is this advice given because *they* want to feel useful?
- Do they themselves want advice but are afraid to ask?

Sometimes I don't have the energy to do any more than nod, but figuring out why someone might be offering advice, often makes the conversations easier.

What should I say when people give me advice and I really don't want it?

It's not always that I don't want to hear advice, it's just sometimes I need to process my own thoughts first.

On the rare occasions when someone has given me advice that has made me feel judged, or was really unhelpful, I have felt it important to say something – not only for my sake but also because I don't want them to make someone else feel judged too.

The more confident I have become in my parenting, the more confident I have been in politely saying, 'I don't need any advice – but thank you.' I have found this preferable to simply listening and not feeling great about the way I'm doing things.

Pete says...

I've received far less advice than Annie has, but in the moments when people have tried to be helpful, either I've smiled and nodded, or, in my weaker moments, given a curt answer back, and then had apologise and admit that, as a new parent, my fatigue got the better of me. When I'm the one giving advice, I catch myself by having a conversation internally: 'Pete, you find receiving advice really annoying sometimes. Does this person need to hear it? Is that actually helpful or are you trying to look helpful, as if you've got it all together? Did they even ask for it?' I think that it's a myth that men only talk about things when they're asking for help to fix something, eg 'My kid doesn't like having a bath. What do you suggest?' Sometimes, with male friends, we have solution-finding conversations but sometimes I know they just want to be heard, received well and have someone simply sit alongside them in their journey of parenthood.

There is a difference between sharing opinions and sharing our experiences

I am so grateful to my mum for her approach to parenting advice, and for how she supported our desire to figure things out for ourselves. She has never told me how I *should* be doing things, and when I do ask her for advice, she'll tell me what worked for her, or what she's seen work, rather than what I should do. Never for a moment has she made me feel like I'm not doing a good job. When I'm struggling, it helps to be with someone who listens and makes me feel heard and loved rather than someone who tells me where I am going wrong.

There is a difference between sharing opinions and sharing experiences. Sometimes our tone, when we give advice, can seem judgmental, even when we don't mean it that way. But when we humbly share our experiences we're able to put them out there for someone to take or leave them.

It might not be possible to start re-educating all the advice givers, but I do think we can model how we want to be given advice. When we do that, we can also make our friends and family feel more loved and supported by the way we listen and share with them.

Often our initial impulse when we see someone struggling is to want to fix it, but how about listening first?

Before leaping to give advice, say, 'Yeah, it sucks doesn't it?' or 'You're doing such a good job.' Then, if they are open to advice, we can think about what might be most helpful to share. Perhaps by saying, 'This is something that worked for me...', 'I love this website...' or, 'Someone told me about this method they tried...'. It's only a simple change in language but it's hugely empowering as there's no expectation for the person listening to have to reveal what they're doing or not doing, or for them to feel obliged to take your advice.

Finding good advice can be tricky

My health visitor strongly advised me to breastfeed, leaving me in no doubt that she wouldn't approve of the bottle of formula we gave our firstborn every now and then. So when I had mastitis and really needed a physical break, I lied and said he was still exclusively breastfed. I didn't feel confident enough in myself as a new parent to be honest. I felt judged and like I needed to lie. Looking back, I'd do that conversation differently. I'd want to be honest and say that I was finding it hard but I believed that the choices we were making were right for us.

Looking back on the days of breastfeeding Big brother, I felt such pressure to keep it up even though I was really struggling because all I was hearing was how important it was. If I had chosen to stop breastfeeding sooner, it may have benefitted my mental and physical health, and Big brother would still have been OK. Now I try not to make choices based on other's judgment and am unashamedly honest about the choices I'm making regarding myself and my family.

If advice makes you feel bad about yourself then it's worth seeking out help from elsewhere. I'm not saying that we shouldn't listen to any advice we don't like. Sometimes we may be given advice that we really do need to hear, perhaps from a doctor or a close friend. However, it's good to remember that we can weigh up the opinion-based advice and throw it out if it doesn't work for us! When I need help, I follow James' advice and go first to God.

> 'If you don't know what you're doing, pray to the Father. He loves to help. You'll get his help, and won't be condescended to when you ask for it.'
>
> James 1:5 (*The Message*)

God made me and my children, and He made me their mother. I trust Him for peace and I ask Him for confidence in figuring out how to parent my kids. Secondly, Pete and I are parenting together so I go to him to chat about how we're doing something. Thirdly, I find wise friends who will listen to me, share their stories and answer my direct questions. Fourthly, I've found some online groups and social media helpful. Being able to post a question and then read back the answers at my leisure, ignoring those that don't help and spending time looking into those that do, has been a really valuable way for me to think through things.

Finding good advice will be different for each of us, and I've found that I have to keep reassessing. The people to whom I asked my baby questions aren't necessarily the same ones I go to for toddler questions, and I know that this may well change again. I also read things, or follow channels on social media, that I really love for a season but that don't work for me in the next. It's OK to change our minds. What's important is knowing that we have choices. We don't have to sit and listen to unsolicited advice, and we can ignore unhelpful posts on social media. We don't have to feel judged. Instead we can seek advice that helps us feel supported and equipped.

Pete says...

Interestingly, I enjoy the process of figuring parenting out, but sometimes I feel out of my depth and need more help. I would usually go first to Annie for advice as she knows our kids best and spends more time with them than I do. She knows the signs when something is up with them and what might support them best. When I'm curious about something I'll either search online or ask a fellow father who might be a few years ahead of me. I'll just go ahead and ask the question – which goes against the myth that men never ask for directions.

The best bit of advice I've ever had was from a friend who told me their 'labour story' a few weeks before our own firstborn was due. I was helping him move house late at night, when he suddenly said, 'Right... so... labour... I feel like I need to let you know about a few things...' and proceeded to tell me about his experience and some of the complications surrounding the birth of their first child. Honestly, it was really what I needed. I'd attended various classes, some with Annie and one on my own, and I felt I was flying in a little blind. Their story helped inform me of some of the realities of childbirth, and set me up to be prepared for whatever might come our way. We have our own story of what happened first and second time around, but that moment, in the van at midnight, was genuinely one of the most helpful pieces of advice I've received.

As we discover what parenthood looks like, we have an amazing opportunity to love and take time to listen to each other. I don't have all the answers and I'm not qualified to give advice because, as I'm discovering now, many of the things I thought I'd mastered with my first baby do not seem to work with my second!

But I do I hope that sharing my stories – the things that have worked for me and the things that really haven't – will help others on their journey to figuring out what parenthood looks like for them.

THINKING HONESTLY

Who gives you the best advice?

Do you need to reassess where you go for advice?

10

Ways kids are like puppies

My brother and I grew up owning dogs as pets, and I hope, one day, we'll get one of our own, but I've come to realise that having kids is pretty similar – so here are ten reasons why we *won't* be getting a dog just yet.

1 They stand at the back door and whine to be let out. You walk into the room, and they turn around and look at you with their big 'puppy dog eyes'; if you don't let them out, they sulk.

2 They dribble everywhere – over your clothes, your hair, your stuff... And they lick your face.

3 They are *always* hungry. They look up after every meal expectant for more, and *always* have room for another biscuit.

4 They create mess. You will spend much of your time cleaning up after them – poo, wee, vomit, toys, dirt... all day, every day.

5 They will chew anything – paper, shoes, the furniture...

6   They can fall asleep anywhere. But after just a short nap, they will be running around again.

7   They need to be toilet trained. It's messy. They love weeing in the garden, but they also love weeing in the house. Let's be honest, they love weeing anywhere! And, just when you think you've cracked the toilet training, they wee on the floor again.

8   They have sharp little teeth. You'll learn pretty quickly not to put your fingers near their mouths. They can't resist nibbling on a finger.

9   They have an incredible ability to find hidden or forgotten about food. Whether it's at the bottom of your handbag or under the sofa, they'll find it – and when you leave to hide the confiscated food, you can guarantee they'll find some more before you're back.

10   They are so cute and cuddly – in spite of all the above – that you readily forgive them for all the poo and chewing!

Sure, in the moment, you may wonder why you ever thought having one of these was a good idea, but at the end of the day, when you're watching them sleep peacefully and you're stroking their smooth little faces, you know you wouldn't trade them for the world.

Coping with illness

This chapter begins with a warning: it contains a lot of poo and vomit. (Well, not literally. That would be disgusting.) So if you would rather not read some particularly graphic childhood illness stories, you might like to skip some pages!

There's no way to sugar (free) coat it – when my kids are ill, it's miserable. But while I might be tempted to wallow in the misery of it, I have found that it can be encouraging to share those particularly miserable days with others so I know I'm not alone. I hope that you too will be able to read these stories and think, *I've been there. It's rubbish. But I got through it.* So amidst all the sick and snot, there will also be plenty of doses of hope and gratitude, making you feel like you've had a taste of that strawberry-flavoured medicine kept in many bathroom cabinets and essential for all parents.

So, here goes...

It seems as if our children's bodies time being ill just when we're planning something special like going to see friends we haven't seen for ages, or an important work event.

One summer we were at a Christian holiday conference where Pete was leading the worship. On the way to the venue, Big brother had vomited but had otherwise seemed fine. We hoped desperately that it was just travel sickness, but just before bedtime, his symptoms confirmed that it wasn't. Cue a very sad evening with him sat on the toilet and lots of night-time nappy changing. Poor kid. The next day we were quarantined. (The conference is based at a boarding school so they have an on-site sick bay with four single hospital-style rooms.) We needed to be quarantined until 48 hours after his tummy bug finished, meaning that, at first, it was for an indefinite period of time. The waiting was horrid, especially once Big brother felt better and started to ask, 'When can I go back to my group?'

I would have admitted defeat and taken the boys home, but driving three hours back then returning to collect Pete only a few days later wasn't something I fancied much either. While Pete skipped off to lead worship (I know he didn't really but it was very hard to be left behind), I sat alone on my plastic-sheeted hospital bed with my signal-less phone and I cried.

We were finally released from quarantine for the last few days of the conference, and Big brother has only fond memories of the week (including the sick bay's cardboard sick bowls, which he thought were 'lovely hats'). Nonetheless, it was a rough week.

This unhelpful timing isn't restricted to Big brother: Little brother has the same skill when it comes to sickness. Just before another event the following summer, Little brother came down with a horrible virus with a fever so he had to stay home with Pete. After arriving home late at night, we didn't manage to settle Little brother until 5.16am and were then awake with Big brother at 7am. It took us all a while to recover.

When your kids are sick it can be a hard slog. Even the unpredictability can be stressful. How poorly will they be? How long is this going to last? Do I need to cancel this event or, even worse, our holiday? How many of us will catch this bug? When our kids are down it's hard not to feel like we're down too.

Pete says...

I wish I could say I had 'skipped off to lead worship' while Big brother was ill but in fact I was a wreck, and some of that emotion and vulnerability came out a couple of times when leading. In fact, I almost swore while sharing what I'd been learning through the week. I don't like it when my family get ill. I'm someone who likes to fix things, so when things are out of my control, I really struggle to cope. Many times, I've had to remind myself not to get frustrated or annoyed when plans haven't worked out due to sickness. Fortunately, my work allows a degree of flexibility, on the days when I do have to go to work and one or both of the boys are ill, it is extremely heart-wrenching to have to leave Annie at home in the midst of it all.

No matter how much I wash the kids' hands, they get dirty again almost instantly. I have friends who anti-bac religiously. I usually carry some anti-bacterial gel in my bag but I generally forget to use it. Stopping them putting things in their mouth is impossible, and, unless we become recluses, they are going to mix regularly with other kids who may be carrying some sort of virus.

I give the boys vitamins (although not as often as I told the health visitor I do) and I try to feed them healthy food, but I have come to the conclusion that they will get sick occasionally. For me, knowing that I really cannot completely prevent illness is less stressful. And, anyway, I've never met anyone who successfully anti-bac'd their children into being healthy all the time – kids will get ill.

There aren't many days in our house where no one has a cold; hopefully though this means that my children will be healthy adults due to the amazing immune systems they must be building. I've reached the point where I wear snot like a badge of honour on my clothes and I even (fairly regularly) use my own (or even the kids') clothes to wipe snotty noses. In the midst of stinking colds and snotty noses it's easy to feel glum but when your kid catches something worse, you realise the cold really wasn't all that bad.

Big brother used to projectile vomit every time he was about to get a new tooth, so we got used to vomit in our house pretty quickly. Once I was driving home from a baby shower and he projectile vomited everywhere. It was awful. I stopped, stripped him down, changed him, wet-wiped the car as best I could and I tried to rush home. Ten minutes from home he did it again. I'd run out of clothes for him, so I just kept going and started the epic clean-up job when we arrived. Fortunately, I didn't have to deal with the lingering vomit smell for the next couple of weeks because the car wasn't mine – it was my mum's!

It would almost be OK if you knew that a sickness bug would pass quickly, so that you could get on with life again, but so often they catch one illness after another. Or, one kid gets better only for the other kid to catch it.

One year we had a toddler with hand, foot and mouth disease on Christmas Day, two diarrhoea and vomiting bugs in January (one of which was shared with me), a horrible stinking cold (again, shared with me) and then chickenpox – all before February. More recently we had a week of a toddler with a fever and a baby who wanted entertaining followed by a week of a baby with a fever and a toddler (whose energy was fully back) who wanted to go outside. There are definitely times when caring for sick children can feel never ending. And then there are other times when you feel like A & E is your second home.

Big brother loves going to the hospital (or 'the play doctor' as he calls it) because they have such good toys. We haven't actually been that often but when Little brother was only a week old, we made two trips to A & E in a day – one for each child.

In the morning, Pete had gone downstairs to find Big brother sat with an open bottle of liquid antihistamine proudly announcing, 'I having medicine Daddy.' After a quick call to NHS 111, Pete was told to take Big brother to A & E. After waiting for a few hours, he was eventually seen by a doctor who was a bit baffled as to why Pete had come in as Big brother seemed fine and probably hadn't drunk much at all.

Later that evening, Little brother, who had a cold, stopped taking his milk and became really difficult to stir. I sat in A & E for hours waiting anxiously, until a doctor finally came to take a look at him – at which point Little brother decided to wake up and feed ravenously!

Only a few weeks later, we were back in A & E again after being told by our local GP to go immediately as Little brother was suffering with another virus. The poor little guy had some pretty full on tests, intravenous antibiotics and had to stay overnight. Those were a tough few weeks. I feel tired just remembering them, but at the time we got on with it and did what we had to do.

I have always been a 'power on through a cold' kind of person. I never expected to have to become a 'power on through a sickness bug or pounding headache' kind of person. This, however, is one of the many joys of parenthood. I almost wish I had given myself permission to lie on the sofa, tissues and hot lemony drinks nearby, and feel sorry for myself when I was ill pre-kids (somehow Pete still finds opportunity to do this nowadays!).

I try really hard not to catch what my kids have. I wash my hands. I offer my cheek instead of my mouth for their snotty kisses. But sometimes I don't turn quick enough to escape them sneezing into my eyeballs. They have both coughed into my mouth on more than one occasion and I have had some pretty horrendous bugs since becoming a parent.

When Pete's paternity leave came to an end, I was nervous about being alone with a less-than-two-week old baby for the first time. Pete had to work an evening, so I figured I would either just sit in front of the telly, or that we'd snuggle up in bed together and get some much needed rest. Instead I got an upset tummy, literally the moment Pete closed the door behind him. I spent the whole evening sat on the toilet feeding my new baby, desperately trying not to squash the little guy as my tummy cramped and I doubled over in pain. It's still a vivid memory but thankfully Big brother won't remember it!

And that wasn't a one-off.

Another evening, Pete being at work, I had just settled Big brother into bed when I started to feel sick. And when I say sick, I mean, really sick. I spent a few hours sitting on the bathroom floor, sweating, shivering and unable to move, until Pete returned and helped me to bed.

Not long after becoming a mum of two, I became really ill again, this time with the flu. All three of us retreated to my bed, where I repeatedly texted Pete to say I needed him to come home early as I physically couldn't manage.

Jesus was born at a time when there was no pink medicine, A & E or antibiotics. Being ill would have been a very different experience and Jesus knew what that was like. His best friend, Lazarus, became ill and died. OK, he was raised back to life, but Jesus understood the misery of sickness (John 11:1–44).

It can be easy to feel as if God doesn't get it but He sent Jesus down into our messy, broken world to feel what we feel. We live in an imperfect world because we walked away from Him. Sickness is inevitable but God is active in the midst of it. He is with us. On those days when we feel at our very worst, our bodies hurt, our hearts are sad or we're desperately worried for our poorly children, God gets it. In fact, there's no one else who understands how we feel more than Him.

'I have indeed seen the oppression of my people... I have heard their groaning and have come down to set them free.' Acts 7:34

God came to be with us in the midst of our pain. He hears us, and He's with us.

As a parent, you can feel helpless when your children are ill and the idea of casting all your cares and burdens on to Jesus really helps in those times. I can soothe, love and give medicine but knowing the Lord has made their bodies means I'm not on my own in caring for them. **Emma**

There is no doubt about it: parenting a poorly kid is the worst. But, even in the lows of tummy bugs and teething, colds and visits to the hospital, being a parent is a privilege. We get to be there for our kids in a way that no one else can. We get to be the person they want; the person they need. We get to be the person holding and comforting our children. We get to say to them, 'I know you're sad; I know you're hurting,' while soothing them and helping them calm down. We get to sing to them while they sob themselves to sleep.

Being a parent can be exhausting. It can feel lonely. Some days it can feel like the ugly, messy bits of parenthood outweigh the good. But even on the messiest days, I am incredibly grateful that I get to be mum to my two boys. It's an honour to be the person they want when they feel hopeless, tired or sick.

Your kids need you. Even when you're covered in poo, vomit, food or whatever else has been thrown at you, and you're not sure what you're supposed to be doing, you're who your kid needs. You get to be that person for them.

Big brother is not really one for cuddling. He's starting to change but usually you only get cuddles when he is ill. It feels weird to enjoy your child's cuddles because he's unwell but I will take any cuddles I can get. I have learnt that cuddling him and letting him know he is loved and cared for is more important than the pile of washing in front of the machine, or the food still on the floor from breakfast yesterday (or quite possibly from the day before). I tell myself I'll get on top of those things but, three years in, I haven't managed it yet! It doesn't matter. Impacting both our hearts with love in those quiet, cuddly moments is more important than seeing the results of tidying.

I was unwell while Pete was away for a weekend and a friend of mine collected both boys and had them all day. It was amazing and possibly the most rest I'd had in the last few years! We all know how rough it is when our kids are ill, so finding people who get that and can provide practical support has been invaluable for me. I've learnt to take any help I'm offered. I don't have to power on through without support. If friends offer to take my kids, or pop to the shops for us, then I say yes! I would do exactly the same for them if they were in need. And when we're all ill, and don't want anyone to catch whatever we have, we can ask our caring friends to pray for us. So let's expect times of illness, try to embrace them, and be grateful that we have family and friends to care for us.

THINKING HONESTLY

In the mess that you might be facing today, what do you feel grateful for?

What do you get to do when your kid is sick that no one else does?

10

Ways to get a kid's attention

Me: 'How was your day, buddy?'
Me: 'Can you hear me?'
Me: 'Oh, I had a really good day, thank you for asking.'

Ever feel like sometimes you're talking to yourself? Getting our kids to pay attention to us can occasionally feel like a real battle. Even saying their name is not always an effective method – no matter if you do say it over and over and over again. I have, however, found ways to get my kids to come running.

1   Walk to the other end of the house. Close the doors. Turn the TV or radio up loud. Then, open a packet of food. Kids are particularly good at hearing crisps and chocolate. Mine would probably hear those even if I was at the end of the garden.

2   To be honest, just open a cupboard or the fridge. Even before you rustle the packet, they'll know you're looking at food. I sometimes wonder if mine can actually hear me think about food.

3 Sit on the toilet. As soon as you sit down, you'll be sure to hear them thudding down the hall towards you.

4 Pick up a laptop, phone, iPad or any kind of device and they'll be desperate to see what's on the screen.

5 Perhaps you want to put some recycling out quickly? Simply turn the key in the door and you'll hear them shout, 'Where are you going, Mummy?' as they come running to join you.

6 Make all sorts of noise in your room throughout the evening and they won't wake, but as soon you want to sleep, simply slide under the duvet, without making a sound, and your little one will be sure to stir.

7 Pick up any dangerous item, a knife, scissors or garden shears, and they will be sure to want to 'join in'. (Note: it must be dangerous for a toddler. It doesn't work with those blunt children's scissors.)

8 Drop the TV remote on the floor by mistake. Toddlers know the sound of a remote and will appear in the hope that they'll get to watch TV. The only downside here is that it will be the TV that has their attention, not you.

9 Click a stair-gate or door shut. If your kid thinks that you're going somewhere inaccessible to them, they will want to join you immediately.

10 Move their highchair or a chair at the table. It doesn't matter if it's nowhere near a meal time, if you touch a chair they will come, expectant for food.

I write this list as a mum of little ones. Who knows what I'm going to do when my boys are teens and most of this won't work. I'd like to think that food will still get their attention but then they'll be able to reach the cupboards, so perhaps they'll have no need for me at all!

Will I ever not feel tired again?

I don't usually wear much make-up but since having children, I wear more in an attempt to look more put together than I actually feel. Recently I thought to myself, *Hey, I'm confident enough to go out without make-up today*, so I just washed my face and out I went. Within ten minutes of leaving the house, I saw someone I knew. They looked at me, clearly trying to hide their horror, and said, 'Wow, you look tired. How are you?' Actually, I was feeling pretty chirpy up until that point.

Once back home, I looked in the mirror and thought *Gosh, I do look quite tired*. In that moment, I realised that this was probably my face from now on. Three years into motherhood and the under-eye bags have become a permanent feature, no matter how much concealer I plaster on. Will I ever not feel, or look, tired again?

Before I had kids, I had no idea that it was possible to function on so little sleep. Or that it was even possible to feel this tired. Sometimes at the end of a day, I really don't know how I managed to get through it. Other days, I sneak to the toilet to rest my head on the cool wall and close my eyes just for a few moments to try to find the energy to carry on. Even on days where I feel like I'm doing OK and powering on through, it's like my brain can't quite keep up. I have lost count of the silly things I've done or said because I've been tired. Dressing Big brother recently, I said to him, frantically pointing, 'I need your... I need your... What are these called again?' He stared back at me, puzzled, and answered, 'Legs, Mummy.'

I worried that perhaps I was alone; perhaps everyone else managed to cope with the tiredness. So I asked around and I am relieved to discover that I was very much *not* alone.

Here is a list of things I and other parents have done due to sleep deprivation. Read it safe in the knowledge that you are not alone: all parents are jolly tired too, even if they seem to be able to hide it.

- Taken the buggy out of the house without the baby.
- Put a dishwasher tablet in a cup instead of a teabag.
- Made tea with cold water and not realised until I've started drinking it.
- Woken up in a panic, thinking that I needed to get to work only to realise it was a Saturday or the evening.
- Felt really proud of myself for getting my kid nicely dressed and off to church on time only to discover, three hours later, that my son's shoes didn't match.
- Raced back into the supermarket in a panic, thinking that I'd left my phone behind before realising I was talking on it.
- Put tantruming toddler in the car seat, got in the car myself and did up my seat belt, only to realise the baby is still on the pavement in their car seat.

- Taken toddler's dinner out of the freezer to defrost, feeling super organised, but at dinner time realised it was porridge.
- Driven the wrong way up a one-way street and not realised until I was shouted at by an oncoming driver – twice in one week.
- Locked myself out and had to put my three-year-old through the toilet window to get the door keys.
- Wrote 'Lots of love' at the end of an email to a manager at work instead of 'Kind regards'.
- Felt a crispy patch in my hair, during a work meeting, and remembered my baby had vomited on my head but I'd forgotten to wash it out.
- Called one of my children 'carrots' instead of his name.
- Shaved only one armpit – the other one is now seriously hairy.

And my personal favourite:

- Half asleep one night, I was about to breastfeed the little bundle I was holding, when I realised I was cradling the dog!

The tiredness competition in our house goes something like this:

Me: 'I'm so tired.'

Pete: 'I can hardly lift my arms.'

Me: 'My eyes hurt.'

Pete: 'My head hurts.'

Anyone else regularly compete in the 'Who's the most tired competition'? If you're parenting with a partner, the likelihood is that *both* of you are tired.

People say, 'I slept like a baby,' and I think, *What a terrible thought!* Sleeping like a baby doesn't conjure up the image of a good night's sleep for me. I prefer the expression, 'I slept like my husband.' Pete has an ability to fall asleep instantly while I'm still lying there, brain-whirring, processing the day. Not only that, he can sleep through our boys waking up, particularly during the newborn phase – the cries did not stir him one bit! He's also a very convincing sleep talker. He will say, 'Yes, I'm awake. I'll go now,' and then roll over. In the morning, he won't remember a thing. We always try to share the nightshift but ultimately if milk is required or 'MUMMY, I MISS MUMMY!' is being shouted in the early hours, it's hard to send Pete.

Pete says...

The early days were brutal. Normally I can sleep through most noises, but those early weeks and months of Big brother's arrival were tough. I didn't quite know what to expect or what I had got myself into. The first nights of paternity leave were great, but very soon, we had to come up with some kind of plan to get through the initial stages. Second time around was a lot harder. We'd moved house a week earlier, and I'd finally taken and passed my driving test. Safe to say we packed a lot into those

> preceding weeks, and it definitely took its toll on me. I struggled to bounce back like I did with our first.
>
> If I was to offer any advice it would be this: it's a marathon, not a sprint. Be kind to yourself in those early days of newborn. You will appreciate it later.

Throughout history, sleep deprivation has been used as a form of torture. Sometimes we dismiss lack of sleep as something we need to cope with during parenthood but the reality is that loss of sleep impacts us in a multitude of ways.

One survey found that new parents are losing around three hours of sleep every night in their child's first year.[1] That adds up to a loss of almost 46 days of sleep – 46 days?! That's more than a month's sleep out of a full year. (If you want to have a good laugh then have a look online at health websites[2] at how to 'repay your sleep debt'. DO NOT read the effects of sleep deprivation on your body – absolutely terrifying. Instead read the bits where it says things like, 'To catch up on sleep debt, you need to get at least two extra hours a night,' or 'Do not set an alarm to wake you in the morning for at least a couple of weeks.' Good one!)

Unless you had some kind of magical unicorn baby who was an excellent sleeper from day one, then no doubt you will have experienced some of the extreme tiredness I'm talking about. There's the night-time feeding, the teething, the times when they were poorly and the nights where you never figured out what was wrong but no matter what you tried they just would not sleep! It's not possible to do parenthood without some sleepless nights.

The average adult needs seven to nine hours of sleep every night. A parent of a newborn might only be sleeping a couple of hours a night. But it's not only the newborn phase that's tiring. They don't turn one and always sleep through the night.

We were fortunate to have a first baby who was a fairly reliable sleeper. However, now that he's three, I realise that's not the end of the sleep story. As a baby, he never came into our bed but now he appears regularly in the early hours. And despite our rule of, 'You sleep in your own bed' when it's 4am and we've just been woken from a deep sleep, it's really hard to return him to his room. Plus, we really don't want him to wake his brother because two wide awake kids will decide that it's playtime regardless of the hour. The main problem with him being in our bed is that he's a really affectionate sleeper and he likes to cuddle or lie literally on top of your face. It's not conducive to sleep at all.

When baby number two came along, I have to admit to being a bit shocked because he wasn't such a reliable sleeper as Big brother. I had definitely forgotten how tiring that phase is. Children know when you're tired. Ours have an ability to sense, through a closed door down the hallway, the exact moment that I close my eyes and start to drift off to sleep − if I wasn't so exhausted, I might even be impressed.

Big brother likes me to be awake and paying full attention *all the time*. Even if he's playing his own game and has asked me *not* to join in. If my eyelids droop for even a moment on the sofa, he will jump on me and shout, 'WAKE UP!' No amount of pleading, 'but Mummy is really tired,' will stop him. I think he feels very passionately that if he isn't going to have an afternoon nap then neither am I. Pete, on the other hand, seems to be allowed to nap whenever he likes!

Parents of young children like to talk about how tired they are. Instead of starting conversations with weather chat, it's about lack of sleep chat. While I understand that it's a common complaint for parents, I have personally found the best way to cope with being tired is not to dwell on it, or think about how tired I look. (Obviously a long hot bath and a full night's sleep would be a better way to cope but try telling my bath-invading, sleep-stealing children that!)

I'm not pretending I'm not tired because let's face it, when you find your phone in the fridge, it's kind of hard to deny it. Instead I try to focus on the positives of parenting rather than the negatives. Of course, when I'm with other mums, we will probably talk about tiredness at some point but I try hard not to start every conversation that way! We all need friends who we can sit with and just be tired. Friends who will listen if we're exhausted and need to moan but who also understand if we're too tired to even talk about tiredness.

As well as talking about lack of sleep, parents love to talk about how well their babies and toddlers are sleeping. Please, if you have got a baby who is sleeping all through the night every night, don't tell everyone! Firstly, babies are sneaky and they'll hit you with a few bad nights in a row as if to say, 'Don't act like you've got this parenting thing worked out.' Secondly, hearing about how your baby is sleeping through the night makes other parents, who are struggling to get a few hours' sleep, feel absolutely rubbish. Thirdly, when your child starts teething or is ill and *isn't* sleeping, you might not get much sympathy.

I remember a friend calling me once after going to a mother and baby group where everyone was talking about how much sleep their children were getting, and she came home devastated that she was doing something wrong because her child wasn't sleeping. She was exhausted and it was really hard to hear how well everyone else seemed to be doing. When you're sat among a group of mums all saying how well they're doing, you might not have the energy to admit you're not and have to be on the receiving end of advice and sympathy.

One thing I've learnt is that parents don't always tell the truth. 'My baby slept through the night' is open to interpretation. For some, it might mean having them in bed from 7pm – 7am (but it takes a long time, and doesn't happen every night), for others, it might mean their kids are asleep from 11pm – 5am. I've found it reassuring to remember that all babies are different, while a parent may have a magical sleeping unicorn baby right now, when it comes to weaning they may really struggle. Or their baby might hit teething hard, while yours breezes through.

Parenting isn't a tick box activity of things we have to achieve. Some babies sleep well and some don't. It's hard when they don't but it doesn't mean that you're not doing a great job.

Our first baby was a pretty good sleeper, so we thought, 'This is great, let's have another.' I was keen to have them in quick succession as I suffered from hyperemesis (severe nausea and vomiting) and wanted to get the pregnancy stages over with sooner rather than later! Two children under two began well but at eight months old our youngest suddenly decided that 4.30am was the start of the day. He was literally wide awake. We tried everything to get him back to sleep but seldom managed past 5am. He was a dream at self-settling at bedtime, so we couldn't work out how to crack it. This lasted almost 18 months. We found it really challenging. Over time, I found myself totally consumed by how tired I was, and was probably really boring: when people asked how I was, 'Tired' was the default response. It really affected our social lives in the evenings because we never felt up to getting out as it meant missing the opportunity to get a few precious hours of shut-eye. It was a strange blur of total delight at how adorable he was and total exhaustion at how little sleep he was letting us get. He's four now and that phase seems like a life time ago, but it was tough. If you're going through something similar – it will get better! **Katie**

Parenthood *is* tiring. As I write, I'm tired. And I think I haven't felt 'refreshed' for at least a year or two, but I have found ways to handle the tiredness and to try to feel the best I can in this current season. For Pete and me, it's been really important to keep assessing where we're at and figuring out where our priorities are. When Big brother was a baby, I would go to bed with him at 7pm and while it did mean I had some sleep before getting up to feed him in the night, Pete and I found we weren't spending much time together. We realised that it was really important for our relationship that we scheduled in, even if only an hour, time for us to connect as a couple. Our favourite way during this phase was to play a card game or to sit and have a hot drink in the kitchen. There was something about sitting at the kitchen table that helped make that a more intentional time of connection.

Now, with two kids we've found we need time together but also individual time in order for us to get re-energised. This usually means doing something creative, so in an evening, I will often sit and write while Pete records music. We don't really do late nights either. There's mild panic in our house if we realise it's gone past 10.30pm and we're not already in bed.

Being kind to yourself and doing what you need to do to get through is probably applicable to every aspect of parenthood. I've learnt how important it is to choose to do *less* in order to be able to give *more* to my family.

Big brother dropped his naps before Little brother was born. He would maybe do 20 minutes on the sofa but that was it, so there was no point doing much even if they were both asleep at the same time during the day. Big brother and I would watch a film during Little brother's afternoon nap just so I got actually got to stop and sit, or lie down. And, if I was lucky, even close my eyes for a few moments.

How much TV kids should watch can become a hotly debated subject – often with a whole lot of judgment. When the topic arises, I usually stay quiet knowing that some people would not approve of how many hours we'd racked up that week. However, when you're trying to get through the day with a tiny baby and an energetic toddler, and you've only had a few hours' sleep, I personally think who cares if you watch a film or two?! I choose to do what I need to in order to get through a season and look after my kids the best I can.

If you need to stay at home and not do activities for a day to rest, then do it. If you can't face doing baby groups for a while, then don't. I was feeling guilty that my second wasn't getting to go to so many baby focused places, but watching him babble away to his brother I realised he's getting so much stimulation and opportunity to learn simply by being part of whatever we're already doing. Sure, he doesn't get to be weekly draped in colourful ribbons while calming music is played over him, but he seems pretty happy bobbing along in the sling while we chase Big brother around.

My relationship with God completely shifted when I started to chat to Him throughout the day in the midst of what I was doing rather than just in quiet moments alone. If I was exhausted or struggling, I would say, 'God, I'm tired. I'm not sure I can do this,' and in that moment I'd feel Him with me in it. I found I started to tell Him the things I was enjoying, thanking Him for them as they happened, as well as sharing the moments where I struggled. Playing worship music while we eat breakfast has also really helped me to start my day connecting with God, especially when I feel too tired to think and I've just poured water on my cereal.

The prophet Isaiah described God as a shepherd who gathers us up and carries us close, a shepherd who gently guides the ewes with their lambs. What a wonderful picture of how God cares for us. It's one I find deeply comforting in moments of exhaustion.

> 'He tends his flock like a shepherd: He gathers the lambs in his arms and carries them close to his heart; he gently leads those that have young.' Isaiah 40:11

I'd love to say that when our kids reach a certain age we will suddenly feel refreshed and the tiredness will lift, but I am currently still in the depths of baby- and toddler-dom, and I am not convinced there is sleep at the end of the tiredness tunnel. However, I have been assured by other parents that it *does* get better.

If you are currently in the peak of parenthood exhaustion, remember that one day we will be the one waking our kids up. Take a moment now to think about what that's going to be like. Will you open the curtains and shout, in your most sunshine-y voice, 'It's morning!'? Will you jump on them? Or, will you simply sit, on your own, and drink 16 cups of tea? Personally, I'm going to get my own sleep trainer clock and I am going to drag my kids out of bed shouting, 'The sun's up! The sun's up! Come see the sun on my clock! Why are you not up? It's moooooorning!'

I can't wait. Our time will come...

THINKING HONESTLY

Is there anything you could do to allow yourself more moments of rest or refreshment, even if very short, in the midst of busy days?

Are you feeling disconnected from people because of how tired you are?

Is there a way you could reconnect with people in spite of being exhausted?

[1]Meg Riley, 'The First Year of Parenthood: New Parents and Their Sleep Patterns', taken from sleepjunkie.org/new-parents-and-sleep [Accessed October 2019]
[2]Ana Gotter, 'Sleep Debt: Can You Ever Catch Up?' posted 2 January 2019, taken from greatest.com [Accessed October 2019]

My body has changed

Big brother: 'Mummy, your tummy is wobbly like a jelly.'
Little brother: *Stares at me inquisitively as I get out of the shower then toddles away, laughing to himself.*
Big brother: 'Ooh, Mummy. Why are your legs not smooth?'

Remaining positive about my body is tricky when my children say and do things like this. And their comments are not just directed towards me.

Big brother: 'Daddy, why have you got a spot on your face?'
Little brother: *Screams and runs away as Pete kisses him with a stubbly face.*

I knew that my body would change when I became a mum, but I wasn't prepared for the fact that these little people were going to talk so honestly – and frequently – about my body. Kids have no filter. Sometimes, this is deeply refreshing. Sometimes however, it's downright offensive!

The reality of pregnancy and having a baby means that my figure *is* different from how it was before. I can blame the stretch marks, and the way that my body holds weight slightly differently, on the fact that it made a human.

However, the reason why I might weigh more than I used to is probably down to the extra snacks and the fact that my exercise nowadays is usually chasing my toddler (which is tiring but not the same as the twice weekly exercise classes I used to attend).

Pre-pregnancy, I didn't really have a sweet tooth – I'd have always opted for a savoury snack – but now I eat a lot more cake than I used to. I could happily eat cake every day. (Full disclosure: I'm actually eating a piece of chocolate cake right now.) Perhaps tiredness makes me crave sugar, or my tastes have changed, who knows? All I know is that my body is different and so are my eating habits.

Please know that I still eat plenty of cake, and plan to carry on doing so, while I'm on my journey of learning to love my body. So don't worry, this is not a chapter all about how to ditch the cake because I'm not up for that.

I'm also finding that as I age, it's getting harder to decipher which changes are down to parenthood and which are simply because I'm getting older. Are those extra frown lines just because I'm ageing or is it from trying to figure out what my kid is saying every day? Are my legs aching because I've been on my feet all day or are they getting a bit more tired anyway these days?

Regardless of where the blame lies, I know one thing for sure: my body has changed.

My journey towards body confidence has been long – and is definitely still ongoing. Even while writing this book, the inevitable increase in snacking and decrease in exercise has had an effect on my body and how I feel about it. I don't profess to have figured out how to have total body confidence because honestly I have good days and bad days but it is something I am consciously working on.

I have realised over the last few years that how I feel about my body is much more than what size I am. I've got tufts of baby hair all over my head from where it fell out post-pregnancy, and I'm pretty sure my body hair grows more than ever before. It can also be hard to love my body when my back is sore, I have joint pain or my sensitive skin is acting up.

The truth is my children aren't my biggest critics. I am. No matter what size my body is, I can find a way to criticise it. When I look at photos of me before children, I can't believe that I used to think I was fat. My insecurities about my body aren't new, it's just that now my lovely children make innocent comments about my body out loud.

After Little brother was born, I thought I was feeling pretty confident about my body until my first evening out where I wanted to dress 'nice'. As I tried on item after item, discovering that nothing fitted how I hoped it would, I ended up emptying the entire contents of my wardrobe out on to the bed. I felt ugly and fat – and I cried.

When I was pregnant, I felt like there was a lot of pressure to lose weight again quickly. I had friends who were buying belly bands (even in the early stages of pregnancy) to wear after they'd had their baby in order to 'get their figure back', and others who forked out for expensive gym memberships, so they could get exercising as soon as possible.

It wasn't necessarily being said out loud but there was a subtle expectation that you were supposed to get back into your pre-pregnancy clothes pretty quickly. I'm usually one for ignoring celebrity culture in the media but I read a lot more magazines when I was pregnant, which included comments about certain celebs losing their baby weight. After my baby was born, when people said, 'Wow, you're looking good,' instead of it making me feel good about myself, it made me think, *Well, clearly they're noticing how I look and have an opinion.* The pressure of looking good was added to all the other pressures I was feeling: needing to rest, focusing on the baby and all the other things I'd begun to juggle.

When I started to think about how I might attain an 'ideal' body shape, I realised I honestly couldn't be bothered. I didn't have the time or money to go to the gym, and I didn't want to eat a restrictive diet different to what my kids were eating. I wanted to be healthier but I didn't want to be constricted by the need to look a certain way. I had so much more to focus on like my kids and my marriage; worrying about dieting or exercise really felt like it should be the least of my worries. I couldn't be bothered and I wanted to be OK with that. I wanted to ditch the pressure.

In Romans 12:1–2, Paul says, 'offer your bodies as a living sacrifice, holy and pleasing to God – this is your true and proper worship. Do not conform to the pattern of this world, but be transformed by the renewing of your mind.'

For me, mind and body are equally important. I need to care for the body God gave me but also to look after my mind and protect it from the way the world thinks.

Being positive about my body isn't just important for me. When I started to think about how I viewed my body, I also thought about my negative habits and self-talk. I realised that what I say about myself, my kids might hear and believe to be true. They don't know about my internal struggle or the fact I'm working on body positivity. They just hear negativity.

The answer isn't necessarily to always pour out praise and compliments on ourselves and our kids but to work on looking after, and caring for, our bodies *and* minds, helping our kids to learn to do the same.

So, how can we do this?

In our house we have a rule. You're not allowed to look in a mirror and comment on your body in a negative way unless you also say what you plan to do about it. This is partly because we're really determined to raise kids with healthy attitudes towards their bodies, and partly because we realised that simply being negative about the way we looked wasn't making us feel any better. It challenges us not to say something negative and dwell on that but to focus on how we can care for the body that God gave us.

So I can't look in the mirror and say, 'I feel fat.' But, I can say, 'I feel like I'm not looking after my body, so I'm going to get my Pilates DVD out and start doing that again.' Saying it out loud, also gives each other permission to keep us accountable.

I desperately want my boys to feel happy in their own skins, to marvel at how incredible the human body is and the fact that God made them. And, I also want them to be able to make healthy choices about how to look after their bodies.

So, our rule isn't that you must always say you love your body as it is. Because I know that, as much as I would love that to be the case, I don't always love my body. I also think it's possible to be comfortable in your own skin but at the same time be actively making choices to care for yourself better. My hope is that my kids will learn to do the same.

Pete says...

For me, when I take care of my body, I find that my body also takes care of my mind. It helps bring my whole being back into alignment with what I feel God created me for: to worship Him and give Him praise.

I love cycling. I love exploring areas and seeing the beauty of both creation and what we have created to fit into the landscapes. I love a smooth road. (It's sad I know but I often comment on the smoothness of roads when driving and ask Annie to note down where we are so that I might explore and enjoy the smoothness of the road again on my bike!) I love pushing my body to do things better or faster. I love it so much that, when I haven't been doing it for a while, I get really down, and everything is affected – work, family, desire to see friends and sometimes even faith.

It's not helpful to think negatively of yourself and your body, but it's not helpful to be unrealistic about your physical abilities either. I've certainly learnt the cost in wanting to feel invincible on the road. At the start of 2019, I came off my bike at speed down a hill. It was reckless and dangerous. I wasn't able to ride for about four months, and for the first month, I couldn't play the guitar or even barely stand. I had a bandage on my finger for six months following the accident and I couldn't drive for a while. That accident had repercussions on my mental health. I despised myself for making such a silly decision, and carried the guilt and shame of that decision for a long time. In turn, I found making decisions very difficult. I still struggle with going down hills and sometimes I feel fear, but through prayer and the support of close friends, I now feel healed of feelings of shame.

I love how Eugene Peterson phrases Jesus' words in Matthew, 'Learn the unforced rhythms of grace. I won't lay anything heavy or ill-fitting on you. Keep company with me and you'll learn to live freely and lightly' (Matt. 11:28–30, *The Message*). I love that phrase, 'the unforced rhythms of grace'. His grace that melodically comes around again and again like a chorus of a song, reminding me to follow Him and live lightly and freely from fear and shame.

Our self-talk is so powerful. It can seem so small and subtle but negative self-talk can take a hold over us. Even if we're talking positively to our kids, it's going to be hard for them to believe it if they overhear us saying something different about ourselves. It's good to reflect on whether we're generally positive or negative about our bodies and ourselves and what our children hear us say out loud.

I made a cake with my little girl recently to prove to her (and myself!) that we can bake. I realised how much my words were impacting her little mind, joking about being a bad baker, not being very good at fixing things, not very organised, because she'd started to quote me to other people, 'Oh, Mummy

*can't do that, we'll have to ask someone else.' I
realised that as much as I tell her that, 'It's always
good to just have a try even if you can't do things
perfectly,' if I model the opposite – I'm not great at
something so I won't even bother to try – she might
grow up thinking only the best is good enough. So
I've decided to keep modelling trying, failing, trying
again, laughing at myself and embracing learning
along the way.* **Jenni**

We have the power to make choices. Every positive choice we make will help our minds to learn new positive ways of thinking.

After my second pregnancy, rather than keeping those clothes that were too small, having them stare at me, taunting me from the wardrobe and hoping that I would eventually fit into them, I donated them to charity shops or sold them on eBay and got myself some jeans in a bigger size. I knew that we were eating fairly healthily (most of the time) because we were conscious of cooking good food for a toddler, and although I wasn't exercising as much as I used to, I was active so I consciously chose to be happy as I was.

There may be times when we do need to lose weight, eat more healthily or exercise more, but what matters more is having a positive mindset about our bodies and food that we can model to our children. The following verses reveal how God carefully created us.

'For you created my inmost being; you knit me together in my mother's womb. I praise you because I am fearfully and wonderfully made; your works are wonderful, I know that full well. My frame was not hidden from you when I was made in the secret place, when I was woven together in the depths of the earth. Your eyes saw my unformed body; all the days ordained for me were written in your book before one of them came to be.'

Psalm 139:13–16

You might like to read these verses to your kids, as well as tell them that God made them and that they are incredible, especially if they don't totally believe it for themselves.

And if *you* are struggling to believe that you are fearfully and wonderfully made, why not ask God to reveal how much He loves you, and read this truth (out loud if you prefer) over and over again:

I am fearfully and wonderfully made.

THINKING HONESTLY

What positive choices could you make to change your mindset and therefore how you feel about your body?

What positive thing could you say out loud about yourself today?

Where do you think any unhelpful pressure about your body comes from, eg magazines or people on social media? Could you unfollow them?

Adding to our number

Another child joining the family unit, through birth (planned or unplanned) or through adoption, changes the dynamic, and can be a challenging prospect.

I've often heard people ask, 'Which jump was hardest? Was it going from no babies to one? One to two? Two to three?' I've not heard anyone ask past that point. Perhaps they're too busy trying to handle the three kids they already have to even think about what adding a fourth might be like!

I wasn't nervous about going through labour again but the thought of having to do pregnancy again was incredibly daunting. I didn't enjoy being pregnant, and when we started thinking about a second baby, I was only just able to imagine facing it again. I was pretty sure I wanted another baby but I felt like I'd just about figured out how to parent one child. He seemed to like me and I enjoyed his company. I wondered if, perhaps we shouldn't ruin it just yet?

Similar to the worries I had when we made the jump from zero to one child, I began to wonder:

Will I love them enough?

Will I be able to give them both enough attention?

Have I prepped Big brother enough?
Am I prepared enough?

Notice the common theme? Can I do *enough*?
Am I *enough*?

If I measure my parenting in 'enoughs', then I will never be doing well because there is always going to be more I could do. Enough is a never-ending measurement.
How about if I take out the word 'enough'?

Will I love them?
Yes.
Will I be able to give them both attention?
Yes.
Have I prepped Big brother?
Yes.
Am I prepared?
Well, can we ever really be fully prepared?!

In reality, once Little brother came along, I didn't have the time, or energy, to ask those questions again. I simply got on with it because I had to.

I worried that Big brother wouldn't be keen on Little brother when he arrived. We talked lots about Little brother before he was born and named him while he was in the womb. I wasn't sure how much Big brother understood but he has been completely besotted with Little brother since he was born. I can still remember his excited face as he first peered at Little brother in his Moses basket, exclaiming, 'A baby! He got a hat!' as he kept putting his hands to his mouth in complete amazement almost not daring to touch the fragile-looking baby in front of him.

I hadn't anticipated how readily Big brother would incorporate Little brother into his daily life; from explaining his favourite TV shows to him (and getting cross when he wouldn't look at the screen) to getting incredibly excited when it came to weaning and helping us pick which foods he should try – sneaking him crisps and chocolate way earlier than I would have chosen!

I can't explain it but they are both more 'themselves' when they are together. They're a little team who I'm sure will gang up on me one day. Daily I try to get the same kind of giggles out of Little brother as Big brother gets from him. I have yet to succeed.

At present, they spend most of their time wrestling each other to the floor. I find myself regularly shouting, 'Be gentle! Get off him!' when Big brother is lying completely on top of Little brother, only to hear Little brother giggling with glee underneath.

However, it's not all happy wrestling and snacking together. The phrase I currently use most is, 'No! We do not bite.' One night we had an early bedtime due to an incident with a metal tin and a big bump to Little brother's head. Sometimes I really struggle to meet both their needs at once, and we all end up pretty hot and bothered.

Adding to our number will look very different for all of us, and I'm sure we will all find different ways of figuring out the new family dynamic. As it turned out, my capacity to love grew even as Little brother grew inside my womb. Never have I felt unable to fully love them both, and I am certain that if we ever add to our number again, we will have more than enough love for them too. It may feel like time, resources or energy are limited but our love certainly is not.

Pete says...

Adding Little brother to our family was both hard and delightful in equal measure. When we had our first baby, we had time to recoup in those early days. But when Little brother was born and Big brother was a toddler, it wasn't possible to rest as much as we had done the first time. However, I found the bond I have with Big brother grew stronger and stronger as we spent more time together, while Annie and Little brother bonded.

My fear was that I wouldn't bond as well with number two. I couldn't have been more wrong. We had ample opportunity to get to know each other. I still spend more time with Big brother than Little brother, due to nap times and nursery drop offs, so I'm aware that Big brother and Annie need to spend quality time together just the two of them. When we carve out one-on-one time with the boys, our relationships deepen and we find that the connection we have with one another is stronger.

The leap from two to four (we had twins) was the hardest especially the first year, which was exhausting! I worry that the oldest two miss out because the babies demand so much of me. I feel like they don't get as much mummy time as they need. They do ask for time with me. I have enough love to go around, no question, but energy and hours in the day are limited! **George**

. . . .

One to two is more than double the work. The impact they have on each other makes parenting even harder. But it's true that your heart just grows when you have another. You don't share or split your love. It's amazing! **Beccy**

My strongest memories of having a little brother are probably the times when he was annoying me. (We do get on well now. Love you, Ed, if you read this!) When he was born, I was seriously unimpressed when my mum presented a brother and not a new baby sister. So I was pretty nervous about how our boys would get on. I'm sure we have many years of squabbles ahead but I honestly could not have anticipated how special their bond would be.

I had such a fear that our first child would feel left out or ignored because I had a newborn to look after. Times when he wanted to read a story, play with me or cuddle couldn't happen because I was feeding or rocking a baby to sleep. It's only now our second is ten months old that I don't have that anymore because they adore each other. To see them laughing and playing together, independently of me, makes my heart sing. **Emma**

People tell you that you'll have extra love for extra kids (true) but I was overwhelmed by the sibling love they have for each other, which no one had mentioned! Each child is a completely different person! I think when we moved to two I had this 'we've done this' mentality. But... er... no, we hadn't because number two was totally different. Treat each one as a precious individual – that would be my advice. **Alistair**

· · · · · · ·

Going from having no children to having two newborn babies (twins) to look after was an enormous challenge. The guilt was absolutely horrible. I wish I'd known to read fewer books and trust my instincts more. I also found sharing with others in the same situation hugely helpful. Going from two to three children was a breeze, though I do sometimes feel guilty about shared attention and the older ones missing out on me. The upside is that seeing sibling relationships is an absolute joy. **Alice**

I realise now what an easy time we had with Big brother. He didn't crawl or climb, instead he went straight to walking. I also appreciate how obedient he was. If we asked him not to touch something, he'd turn around and go do something else. Little brother, on the other hand, is proving to be a pretty proficient climber, thinks it's hilarious to jump off things, and will say, 'No, no, no, no, no,' when we've asked him to stop what he's doing. It's been quite a shock.

> *I think the biggest life change is from zero to one child but then you are up for the challenge and it is two people looking after one child. It was actually a much bigger psychological and physical challenge going from one to two children, realising that what worked with the first child didn't work with the second; that the toddler wanting lots of stimulating playtime would probably want it at exactly the moment child number two wakes; that you really only have one pair of hands; that if child number two sleeps horrendously, it will be a very tiring first year; and that they are temperamentally very different children. My wife would also say that when she was at home with our oldest child, she pretty much got no time to herself at all. In comparison, going from two to three children was a breeze!* **Adrian**

Although we parents have no idea whether our next child will enjoy sleeping or what their temperament will be like, there will be things that aren't new. I may have been completely shocked by the sleepless nights second time around (even though we'd been there only two and a half years earlier) but at least I wasn't starting from scratch when it came to things like changing nappies, baby feeding and having some sort of routine.

I have always been a lover of routine, and although we had to adapt slightly to fit around a toddler *and* a baby, I have found that the days are easier for us because the boys (and I) know what to expect. We aim for set meal times (which inevitably get moved forward), set bedtimes and regularly talking through what is coming up. Big brother seems to feel a real sense of pride helping Little brother with things like inviting him to brush his teeth or to come to the table. He especially values Little brother's nap time where he gets quality time with me or Pete.

I've had anywhere from one to seven kids at a time (I'm a mum, step-mum and foster mum), and honestly the more kids you have the easier it seems to get as they become a team. Saying that, two things have particularly helped me to manage. Firstly, having a solid routine, so that they all know what to expect. I use a chalk board to let them know what jobs need doing and what's coming up that week. Secondly, making sure that there is one-on-one time with every child every week (also planned into the routine), so that they know when their time is coming – and to save up all their venting until then! **Kate**

I am already finding that, when I look after friend's kids, Big brother ends up being entertained more and needing me less as they go off and play together. He regularly plays with our neighbour's child and I find I don't see him for ages, apart from the odd snack request!

I am looking forward to when my kids are a little older and we can do outings with their friends tagging along and things like sleepovers. I remember, as a teen, spending so much time at a friend's house that I was treated like one of their children. Once, during dinner, I giggled during grace and got made to do a lap of the garden before I was allowed to eat!

Having my kid's friends round might free up my time but the house often ends up as a bit of a tip. When we were growing up, my mum was always so welcoming that lots of my friends would end up at our house. Inevitably this meant more noise and mess in the house (which I know she didn't mind) but I loved being at home with my friends. Now that I'm a mum, I hope I can create the same welcoming space for my kids' friends as well as their parents.

We have a friend who has been in hospital recently with her very young baby, and her two older children have really struggled. Physically, she couldn't be with all of them at once and there have been times when all three have needed her. The family has been supported by our church and local community practically and in prayer but it has still been extremely difficult.

Ultimately having more kids *will* be more tiring, more challenging and more difficult to give each child the same amount of attention as when there was just one. However, the blessing of watching sibling relationships grow and building your family is so worth it, and even better when we can do that within community and talk about the challenges together.

To go back to the question I pondered at the start of this chapter: Am I enough?

Ultimately it's a question I don't even need to ask because God is enough.

> 'My grace is enough; it's all you need. My strength comes into its own in your weakness.'
>
> 2 Corinthians 12:9 (*The Message*)

Admitting that we're not enough and that we can't do it on our own is hard but when we do, we can also choose to depend on God because He is more than enough. The joy of following God is that even when we are weak, we can be completely dependent on Him and His power is shown through our weakness. Whether you're adding your first child or your fifth child, I pray that today you would know God's strength and that His grace would be enough for you.

Connecting with our kids

Sometimes parenthood is boring and frustrating. Ever felt like we're not allowed to say that?

Reading the same book over and over again, feeling like we are constantly telling our kids to tidy up or get their shoes on, listening to the same sibling squabble on repeat, or the continuous preparing of more food as if they've never been fed before. Parenthood can be pretty repetitive.

When I first became a parent, and Big brother was small and unable to protest (at least not with words), I got to choose all of the activities. A leisurely stroll to the shops, meeting friends or watching a film of my choosing were all very doable activities. However, Big brother is now more than able to makes his opinion known if my choice of activity is not to his liking.

Some days I get to the point where I honestly cannot face reading the same book again, or playing trains one more time. I admit that I have hidden (and maybe/ definitely given away) toys and books that I have just been completely sick of and then dodged answering where they've gone!

I'm trying to teach my kids that it's OK to be bored. I want them to use their imagination and be comfortable to be sat just with their own thoughts. However, I don't always model this well; I'm not very good at it. When I'm bored, I generally get my phone out to browse social media or make myself a cup of tea. I'm convinced Big brother thinks I wouldn't function without a huge amount of tea – he may well be right.

What I've come to realise is that parenting, on the whole, isn't boring – but parenting without connection is.

Both hearts and minds are talked about lots in the Bible. I don't find it an easy distinction to explain to kids but I do think it's important to talk about our hearts, our feelings, our hopes, our dreams; and our minds, what we're thinking, how we reason and weigh things up. When we talk about our hearts we're exploring something much deeper, really getting into what we're feeling deep down.

We've been able to find a language to talk about connection. I have also found it the simplest way to talk about my relationship with God and how when I worship or chat to Him, my heart connects to His heart. I share daily with my kids how my heart is doing and how I'm feeling, ask them how their hearts are and talk about whether or not we feel connected with one another.

In Proverbs it says, 'Above all else, guard your heart, for everything you do flows from it' (Prov. 4:23). I want my kids to know how important it is to look after their own, and each other's, hearts and I think the best way to start is to help them to be confident about what is going on in their own heart and begin to talk about that.

I know that just thinking about investing more into connection can be tiring, but honestly it's a really small investment for a huge reward. When Big brother and I are disconnected from one another; for example, when I'm trying to get him to put his shoes on for nursery and he's trying to show me something and I'm not paying attention, we both end up feeling frustrated, we both don't listen to each other and we're both unlikely to reach a happy outcome. But when we're connecting well, I feel like I understand him better, his behaviour is much better and if, for some reason, it isn't then I feel able to handle it and talk to him about it – most of the time.

The times when I've said yes to playing cars or trains with him and I've fully invested in creating characters and drama are always times when I've seen him express such deep joy. If I play for 30 minutes completely disinterested then his heart doesn't get full but if I fully invest, even for a few minutes, I get the joy of watching it overflow.

Big brother loves to pretend he's a caterpillar in a towel cocoon after his bath and insists we are completely amazed as we watch 'a beautiful butterfly' emerge. He could re-enact this transformation again and again; I'm usually done after the first time. However, when I take the time to really act out my part as amazed onlooker and let him keep going, it's amazing to see how connected it makes him feel. He's also then happier to go off and play on his own or to agree that we'll play for a bit longer then we'll do something else. It eliminates his frustration and makes him much more open.

Finding connection in parenting isn't only about joining in with the games they want to play, although that definitely helps, it's about finding ways to connect in whatever you're doing.

Pete says...

I've grown to love the word 'connection'. Before Annie and I were married, I found it slightly off-putting; however, this word is great at describing how to be more present. It has also been really useful not only for thinking about what I can do to stay connected with our kids but how to reconcile that disconnect when we've fallen out or done something to upset one another. There are times when our eldest has done or said something to upset me (like 'I wish Daddy wasn't my father'), and I've been able to explain how this made me feel and how it's caused us to be disconnected from one another. This has led to remarkable reconciliation attempts by a toddler and it's challenged me to initiate reconnection with all members of our family when something has come between us, or we've not been connected in such a way that reflects a godly connection.

One of mine and Pete's biggest goals as parents is to raise kids who are comfortable talking about their emotions and feelings, whether they are positive or negative, which is something we really only started to learn to do ourselves as adults, so we'd love to give our kids a head-start. Time spent eating together is often a good opportunity for us to have these conversations. We also try to build them into conversation as much as possible throughout the day by asking questions like:

- How does your heart feel?
- What was something that made you happy/sad/ cross today?
- How do you think that made the other person feel?
- In that story, do you think the two characters felt connected with one another when that happened?

Little brother doesn't have many words yet but we also ask him these questions. Big brother takes it upon himself to interpret his babbled answers. We've created an expectation that we talk about our feelings every day. It's become a normal part of family life for us and the more we do it, the more we see Big brother talking unprompted about connection in everyday life whether that's in his own relationships, in stories or on TV.

As mentioned already, I try to join in with their choice of activity (even when I don't want to). Now, don't get me wrong, I don't do *every* activity Big brother asks me to as it's not possible, especially with a baby around. However, I know that choosing to say yes to some activities will really make his heart happy. For me, bathing with Big brother is a somewhat stressful activity but I know that it brings him joy and it makes him feel really connected to me. So when he asks, I listen and make sure I don't always say no. I also try to ask him first to have a bath with me.

Let me be the first to admit that I will sometimes miss something Big brother wants me to hear or see because I'm distracted. I know that when Pete does this to me, I get really frustrated so why would my kids feel any differently? Choosing to pay attention and listen well is such a simple thing to do for huge heart connection. When I stop and pay proper attention, ensuring he feels heard and that his feelings have been understood, then I can chat to him about what is going on in the moment before he gets frustrated or angry that I'm not listening.

Note: there are times when I will tell him I can't listen or look immediately (eg when I'm in the middle of changing a horrendous pooey nappy) but I explain clearly that I understand how he might be feeling and that I would love to listen to him when I've finished what I'm doing.

Asking Big brother what would make him feel connected or what he wants, in a situation, in terms of my attention has been transformational for us. TV is one of those ways he likes to connect with me. When he's choosing what to watch, I will often ask whether he wants me to watch with him or not. He likes to watch some incredibly boring educational programmes! Honestly, they almost bore me to tears. And he knows I don't love to watch those, so sometimes he'll choose to watch one of those on his own. But on other occasions, he'll try to pick something we'll both enjoy, so we can connect with one another while watching. If he asks me to watch with him then my phone goes down and I pay proper attention, asking questions and listening well to him. It's actually also been a really simple way to teach him to think about how his choices impact others.

Being aware of my kids' love languages has also been really helpful. This idea of love languages is that there are different ways that we give and receive love, and when we know each other's love languages, we can demonstrate love more effectively. In Gary Chapman's book, *The 5 Love Languages*[1] he talks about there being five main expressions of love: words of affirmation, quality time, receiving gifts, acts of service and physical touch. For example, Big brother has never particularly been a physical touch kid. Even as a baby, he'd get really frustrated at being passed around for cuddles and putting him down would often ease his grizzling. However he feels really loved through quality time (like us enjoying TV together) and through receiving gifts. When I surprise him with something when I collect him from nursery, even if it's a tiny token of a gift like a daisy I picked from the grass verge outside, he is just so full of joy. Whereas we can already see with Little brother that physical touch is definitely higher up on his list and a big squeeze brings out the biggest grin on his face.

It's been really fun testing how different languages connect with Big brother, and helping him explore how to show love. He's a real gift giver. Often we've been out shopping, he's seen something and insisted that we *need* to buy it for someone. Helping facilitate him showing love to others has been a real privilege.

Life can be really hectic and it can be easy to let quality connection time slip out of the day. It sometimes helps to plan time for connection. Big brother likes to know what's happening in the week, and each evening he wants to know what's happening 'after this sleep'. We make sure that, as well as listing all the activities coming up, we talk about how we'll have time for connection. Most of our days are 'Mummy, Big and Little brother days', so we'll talk about what we'll do together, and we'll think about how we'll connect with Daddy when he gets home. Our hope is that it's really helping him see relationships as an expected part of the everyday.

This also means that when we're feeling disconnected, we can talk about planning in connection time and looking forward to it; for example, looking forward to a Saturday family day and thinking in advance about what we can do together. We're also realising how important it is to have one-on-one time, and even if Big brother chooses to invite Little brother to join in, I'm trying to plan opportunities for time with each of them individually.

When I'm away overnight for work, or if Pete is working late and not home for tea, then we make sure we check in on FaceTime. Often the boys will be totally nonplussed and prefer to chat to someone else or continue whatever game they were playing. We've found that this means that we're checking in the right amount as they feel connected enough to be happy to do other things. I always remember how my mum used to say that she knew we were OK if she didn't hear from us because that meant we were happy and enjoying life.

Intentionally creating connection makes parenting easier. As well as helping our family relationships, it's helping us all learn how to look after other people's hearts better and to fix things when the connection gets broken. For example, when I get cross at Big brother for not listening and shout at him, he will tell me how it hurt his heart that I shouted (which obviously breaks mine). We then talk about how both of our actions led to us getting hurt and disconnected from one another and then figure out what choices we can both make to fix it.

It doesn't mean we don't struggle or have days where we just don't manage to connect well with each other, but we are on a journey to learn how to do it better every day.

THINKING HONESTLY

How could you connect with your children today?

What are your kids' love languages? How do they give and receive love?

What could you do to make them feel loved today?

[1]Gary Chapman, *The 5 Love Languages* (Chicago, IL, USA: Moody Press, 2009)

Helping our kids through tricky seasons

My granny died on Christmas Day a few years ago. She had been poorly in hospital for a few months but had remained in high spirits. As she died, my mum and I sat beside her bed and I held her hand. It was an incredibly special moment but not one anyone would choose to have as part of their Christmas Day.

Afterwards we went home to have our Christmas dinner as a family and spent much of the time reminiscing about Granny, sharing stories of her life and what she would have been doing if she had been with us. It was overwhelming, and I remember feeling like I just couldn't handle talking about her anymore, so I snuck off to my room. My dad came and knocked on my door to check that I was OK, and I explained (not very articulately) that I needed to not be doing the happy reminiscing thing but wanted time to just feel sad. He told me that was perfectly OK and that he understood.

Although I was an adult, I very much felt like a child in that moment and being given 'permission' by my dad to grieve in the way that worked for me was exactly what I needed. That Christmas Day didn't look anything like how Christmas 'should' be but for us, as a family, we figured out what we needed and we found a way through.

Christmas isn't the only season that can be difficult. We are likely to face all sorts challenging situations: when someone close to us dies or has a long-term illness, we're facing a difficult event or our kids are struggling at school. There's no guidebook for how to navigate these times as a family. We're each on our own journey of figuring out what it looks like for us to be a family, as we love and support each other in our own way.

After reflecting on some tricky seasons in our family, and from conversations with others, I wrote this list of pointers, which I hope may be helpful as you figure out how to equip your family at similar times.

- If you know a season is going to be tough, it might be helpful to find time as a family to think about some simple things you can do to help you cope with the changes around you. Perhaps there are traditions that used to belong to a specific person who's no longer around that you might like to carry on or start new ones.
- Think about whether you and your kids are naturally introverted or extroverted. If you're heading into a time, which might be hectic and full of people, think about how you can help your kids to create space where they need it. You might reassure them that it's OK to go to their rooms if they are feeling a little overwhelmed. Or, if they don't have their own space, think about how to create a quiet area. There might be some task you can involve them with so they have

something to focus on, like laying the table.

- Discuss ways that your family can connect with God in the midst of what is going on.

- Sometimes when we're with lots of people, it can be hard to get much quality time with our kids. Think about ways to give each other focused attention in the midst of busyness.

- Perhaps your kids aren't particularly physically affectionate. Spending time with lots of people can be intrusive on our personal space when there are so many people to greet and then say goodbye to. Maybe think in advance about what your family expectations are, and explain to relatives that your children might not want to kiss or be kissed but that it's nothing personal and you'd rather your children didn't do anything they're not comfortable with. Perhaps you can chat with your kids about different options for goodbyes, like waving, high fives or simply, 'Bye!'

- If you have a difficult family member (and who doesn't!) that your child would rather not interact with, maybe you could tell them beforehand that it's OK for them to sit next to you if they are feeling uncomfortable.

- Sometimes, in tough situations, we can feel that we just need to put on a brave face and do something we don't ideally want to do, but other times we need to choose to prioritise our kids' safety and wellbeing. If you need to spend time with extended family but feel it may not be a very pleasant atmosphere for your children, then maybe think about what boundaries you could put in place; for example, limiting your time

with them or staying at a nearby hotel.
- If a loved one has died, maybe think about how to create space to grieve together as a family and individually; discuss how it's normal to feel sad; figure out ways to celebrate and remember that person and establish that it's OK for us to choose to opt out if we want to.

When the sibling of some children in our church died, I talked through the beautiful description of heaven from visions in the Bible and how Jesus prepares a room for us. I asked them what things they would like in their brother's room and they drew those pictures.
Elaine, children and families pastor

Pete says...

I've found that sometimes as parents it comes down to us to safeguard our children in tricky situations, but where possible to equip our kids to be able to make those kind of decisions for themselves, now and in the future. I hope to be able to lead our family through these seasons with a Christlike attitude, and be the example of Jesus in those moments. In those seasons, I found the most Christlike thing I should do, and want to do, is spend time with God and be with Him before I walk into making any decision that is bigger than what I or anybody else wants. I find that this verse from Isaiah is particularly helpful in tough

> situations: 'So do not fear, for I am with you; do not be dismayed, for I am your God' (Isa. 41:10).

For our family, we try to use easier times to prepare us for the more challenging ones we may face. We hope to equip our boys with the knowledge that God is with them all the time, whatever's going on, so that they have no doubt of His closeness to them when they enter a tricky season. Ultimately, our desire is that they would know God's peace and feel equipped to make good choices for themselves.

Whatever you're facing, now or in the future, I hope that you will be able to create space and opportunity to face it together as a family, figuring out what's right for you for that time.

THINKING HONESTLY

What could you be doing now to equip your kids for times in the future that may be challenging?

Are you going through any tricky situations that you could gently share with your kids to help them learn about the choices you're making?

10

Ways you know your kids are growing up

I've heard lots of friends say they wish their kids weren't growing up so fast, but I'll admit that I normally welcome mine gaining independence and doing things for themselves a bit more. However, there are moments when I think, *Woah, just slow down a minute!*

Here are ten of those times when there's really no denying that they're growing up.

1.   Suddenly they can out-argue you, repeating logic and phrases that they've heard from you.

2.   They start pronouncing words correctly; no longer are we sat in a 'trackick jam' or eating 'cumbububer' for a snack.

3.   They suddenly don't think you're the coolest person in the world. In fact, they make it quite clear they really don't think that anymore.

4.   From one day to the next, their trousers are suddenly skimming their ankles.

5 When you try to help them understand their feelings and they turn your language back on you; for example, when I explained to Big brother that he might be coming into our room at night not because he was scared, but because he felt lonely – cue him appearing at 3am and telling me how incredibly lonely he was.

6 When you ad-lib and skip through a book, only to have them correct you and make you go back and read the pages properly.

7 When you're trying to figure out some kind of technology, and they take over and do it for you.

8 When you spell out a pudding suggestion and they say, 'I want some I-c-e c-r-e-a-m please? Can I go get it from the freezer?'

9 When you're trying to be knowledgeable about something completely obscure and they say, 'Actually Mummy, it's a colossal squid.'

10 When they say that they want to be a fire fighter when they grow up instead of a fire engine.

I'm in my thirties and I still don't feel that grown up, so sometimes I feel a bit of disbelief at how quickly my kids seem to have stopped being babies!

Letting go

The moment we hold our newborn baby in our arms, or cuddle our adopted child, we're not thinking about how one day they'll become an adult and leave home – we're thinking about how we intend to hold them forever, to love them and make sure nothing bad *ever* happens to them.

Thinking about our kids growing up and leaving home can be quite a scary prospect, especially growing up in the world as it is now. But we can't hold their hands forever; we can't wrap them in cotton wool. They *will* eventually go out into the world, so our job as parents is to do our best to equip them with the skills, wisdom and the decision-making abilities that they will need to keep them safe in the world.

How can we find that balance of wanting to help our kids gain independence but also wanting to protect them and keep them safe?

Right now, I'm preparing a one- and three-year-old for the world, and I'm preparing myself to let them go in the future. My journey in this is only just beginning. It may look different in a few years' time, so here I will share where we're at now, and what my hopes and dreams are for their future.

I want my kids to feel equipped to handle things without me because I won't always be there to help them. As much as I don't want them to feel pain or sadness, I do want to coach them *through* it rather than protecting them *from* it. I want to help them learn how to handle emotions and feelings, so that when they experience grief, heartbreak, bullying or hurt, and I'm not there to help them, they know what to do or where to go for help.

I want to equip them with both practical and emotional skills, from the ability to handle finances to being able to look after their mental health when life can feel overwhelming. I don't mean teaching my kids to be adults while they're still growing up but using everyday experiences to help strengthen them for future challenges. We do this at the level they're at rather than letting them feel the full expectation or weight that we do as adults.

I am really passionate about raising emotionally healthy kids who feel comfortable talking about anything and everything. Our aim is to make no topic a *big* topic. Many adults struggle to talk about their emotions, myself included, so my hope is that talking openly will become a lifelong habit and their immediate response to problems when they are adults.

Growing up, I didn't feel comfortable talking about my feelings. I didn't think anyone would be interested in how I felt, and if I did share my feelings, I always apologised for them. It didn't help that I really struggled to identify how I was feeling. I was self-conscious and keen not to draw attention to myself through extremes of emotion, high or low, so I found I moderated my outward display of emotions.

As an adult, I have learnt to actively choose to

acknowledge how I'm feeling and to articulate those feelings. I had the great privilege of working for a charity where I was surrounded by people who helped me through that process. I was encouraged to be honest and vulnerable and spent many days crying. I learnt that sharing openly led to much deeper connection, and that actually no one saw me as weak but instead strong for sharing how I was feeling.

I would love to raise kids who are completely at ease talking about how they feel, who don't need to learn how to do it in adulthood but instead are those adults who can help others feel the same and learn too.

A survey in 2014 found that one in six adults experience symptoms of a common mental health problem every week, and one in five adults has considered taking their own life at some point.[1] This is the reality of the world that our kids are growing up in, and although attitudes are changing, mental health is not a topic that everyone feels comfortable talking about.

When I was at university, I had a period of mild depression. When a doctor offered me anti-depressants, I felt I couldn't take them as I couldn't face telling my family. I didn't know how to talk about it. I didn't want to disappoint my family or for anyone to think I wasn't coping. But then I had some counselling, which was transformative for me. I learnt so much but mainly that asking for help and saying you're not OK is definitely *not* something to be ashamed of. That's what I want my kids to know. That it's OK not to be OK, and that it's OK to ask for help. There is no shame in needing help.

I openly talk about mental health. Even my youngest, who is seven, knows about suicide but that there are so many places to ask for help. They know the signs of depression, and that life can be overwhelming, so talking is the best option. We talk about 'safe ears', people who will listen no matter what, and who those people are. I feel that once that's set in stone, then they can fail at everything else but will never let it overwhelm them.

Also, when we go to the doctors, I make all of the children speak for themselves. Once they have given it their best try, then I will help. I've done this ever since they turned five and started school. **Kate**

. . . .

Even though my girls are still very young, I'm really honest with them about life. They understand in a limited way that sometimes mummy and daddy are sad or sometimes we have to be kind to friends because they are sad. I'm not afraid of saying I've got things wrong. I want them to always know that adults can mess up too. I think it's about starting conversation now at such a young age, so that as they grow, it's natural to share deeply together as a family. **Emma-Louise**

Talking openly can also mean broaching tricky topics such as the human body, sex and relationships. We made a conscious decision while Big brother was still a baby that we wanted to make sure our kids were equipped to use the correct anatomical names when they talked about their bodies and asked questions.

So, when Big brother started asking about his body and our bodies, we told him about penises and vulvas. We've taken an approach of talking honestly about all our body parts, so that, we hope, he learns to do the same and isn't ever embarrassed by it.

Pete says...

Initially I felt uncomfortable using the proper anatomical names for our body parts. I'd always used nicknames as it made it less awkward but Annie and I do want to empower our kids to feel confident about talking about their bodies, especially if something is hurting, and that feels more important than whether I feel awkward.

Recently I was at a walk-in medical centre. As I was waiting for my number to be called, I noticed a father and his son shuffle to the counter to talk to reception. The father was embarrassed to say why they needed an appointment, and quite sheepishly said in a hushed voice, 'My son, he's got a problem with his... bits.' I felt so sorry for them both. Sometimes our bodies don't quite work properly, however I wondered whether the father was also communicating something a lot deeper. Of course, it's natural to feel awkward, however there is no shame in walking into a medical centre, and asking for medical help when we need it. That's the whole point of them. It got me thinking however about all the emotions present in that moment: unease, awkwardness and embarrassment. Sometimes, if we communicate with any of these emotions, it can lead to shame or humiliation. It may not be our intention but that sense of shame or humiliation could result in something much deeper: fear. In a split second, we may have unconsciously begun a strand of fear on the timeline of our children, because we, as parents, are embarrassed or ashamed to be bold and 'call a spade a spade' or in this case 'call a penis a penis'. I don't know what happened to this father and son but I do know what happened in me.

I have a skin condition, which I have often felt ashamed or embarrassed to talk about. I've tried to hide it, and I have felt uncomfortable, in the past, talking about it. However, when equipping my children to talk about their bodies and what is happening to them, I've found that I've also been learning to do this myself. I have felt more confident about talking about what's wrong with my body. I have grown less ashamed of highlighting my body's frailty, less fearful about what others may think and less fearful of rejection. I am reminded of the apostle Paul's words, 'when I am weak, then I am strong' (2 Cor. 12:10). When I am weak, and there's a reason

> for that weakness, somehow, in the difficulty, I find
> an unusual strength to walk in confidence in who I
> am in Christ.

By encouraging our children to learn and talk openly about the human body, we run the risk of them bringing up the topic anywhere. Once in the doctor's surgery waiting room, Big brother was watching an animated video on the TV screen and asked, 'Why is there a penis, Mummy?' (It was an image of a virus or something but it was pretty phallic, to be fair!) I was fascinated by the response in the room: some stifled giggles but others expressed horror. I know people don't expect a three-year-old to say it, but 'penis' isn't a rude word, it's a part of the body and I want him to be comfortable talking about it. We have a selection of books about the human body, which he loves learning facts from, particularly about the heart and bones – he talks about those too but people don't seem so shocked to hear veins or the skull being discussed!

As well as talking about private parts and how males and females are different, we talk about relationships. Recently, we were watching *Into the Woods*[2] and Big brother asked why Cinderella wouldn't kiss her husband, the prince. (For those of you who haven't seen the film, it's because the prince had a brief fling with the baker's wife.) Cue having to try to explain infidelity to a three-year-old. We talked about how daddy had chosen to marry and kiss me, and how if he kissed someone else, it would be hurtful and he'd break the promise he made to kiss only me.

Often, we end up going down a path in a conversation and I think, *Goodness me! I'm going to have to explain something massive here,* but more often than not he loses interest. For example, seeing a couple with a baby:

Big brother: 'Mummy, why do they have a baby?'
Me: 'They wanted one so they made one.'
Big brother: 'No they didn't! God made it.'
Me: 'Well yes, God made the baby using their bodies.'
Big brother: 'Not the daddy's body. Just the mummy's.'
Me: 'Well, actually the daddy's body was also important...'
Big brother: *Runs off to play.*
Me: *Breathes a sigh of relief.*

Since that conversation, he has asked again and now understands that the daddy's body is needed too. Every time he asks questions, we gradually add more layers to his learning, always leaving it open for him to continue the topic of conversation if he wants to, whatever it may be.

The other day, Big brother wandered off in a restaurant, and when I went to fetch him, I overheard his conversation with a slightly shell-shocked waiter:

Big brother: 'Will you die?'
Waiter: 'Erm...'
Big brother: 'Everyone dies.'
Waiter: 'Well yes, I guess I will eventually.'

Working as a funeral pastor means that death is a topic that is talked about regularly in our house. We're keen that it becomes a really normal thing to talk about in our family, not something mysterious or scary as it's inevitable that they will experience someone dying at some point in their lives.

Watching Big brother process his learning through play has been fascinating, not to mention the conversations we've had. Sometimes, when he talks about death so naturally, I have a moment where I wonder if we've made it too normal. He gets that death is sad, he just isn't scared of it, which is ultimately what I wish for him to feel.

Death and loss already feature in so much of what he's seeing and learning, particularly on TV. Watch any Disney film and there's probably an orphan or a scene where someone dies with very little explanation of what's going on, so we've done lots of talking when watching films.

He also asks how old people are and if they'll die soon (usually not in front of them!). Sometimes we say that people die when they get *really* old but he also knows that people can die before they get old. We have talked about this with him following times when friends of ours have died of cancer. I don't want him to be scared of death, thinking that anyone could die at any moment, but I also don't want to shield him from the fact it's not only very old people that die.

We talk very matter of factly about death, about our new bodies in heaven, what happens with our old bodies and how we won't need those anymore. We also talk about someone dying, rather than 'passing away', or 'going to sleep'. Our aim is to make it as clear and easy to understand as possible, and to constantly leave conversation open for our kids to keep asking questions or sharing their thoughts.

We're keen to expose our littles to real world issues, like hunger, material poverty, brokenness, refugees and settlements and not hide or sanitise issues such as death. **Emma**

Many of our conversations about relationships and death naturally lead into a wider conversation about faith. Like everything else, when it comes to faith, I'm always keen that we answer all their questions and tell our kids the truth. It can be easy to think that some parts of the Christian faith are too big for a kid to grasp. But how can we talk about God's incredible love for us without also talking about how people walked away from Him? How can we talk about God's incredible rescue plan without talking about the cross?

Our small snippets of conversation about faith are all part of one bigger conversation. I never feel I need to cram the whole gospel story into a moment but instead to ponder with him as we gradually talk about the whole Bible story over our many conversations. I love Big brother's questions and it's a privilege to be able to answer them but sometimes I try not to launch straight into full on, big answers. I might ask him, 'What do you think?' first (particularly as this clarifies whether his question is about a big topic or not – often it's not).

I've also learnt not to shut conversations down or fob him off with unnecessarily dumbed-down answers. I want to always be truthful. Yes, answers will need to be age appropriate but I'm keen never to tell a lie. If I don't know the answer, I'll tell him. Then we can look for books and resources together or find someone else to ask. I hope that this will mean that he always knows that he can ask me anything and expect me to listen and be honest with him, and that he will know how to go and look for answers when I'm not there to ask.

I'm trying to encourage independence by asking my son to try to do things himself and talking honestly about things as they come up. **Katharine**

I still ask my mum about many of the practical things that come with being an adult.

Me: 'Why do my curtains hang strangely?'
Mum: 'Because you didn't pull the cord to pleat them.'
Me: 'Should we get life insurance?'
Mum: 'Yes.'
Me: 'What's the best thing to do for headlice?'
Mum: 'We used a great tea-tree shampoo when you were little. I'll have a look for some.'

I hope that by the time my kids leave home, I'll know more answers to life's everyday challenges, otherwise I might be directing them to Granny!

When it comes to teaching life skills, we try to invite our kids to join in with what we're doing whenever possible. Big brother has now taken on the weekly responsibility of pushing a little trolley and helping to do our food shop. (While I run along behind, with my trolley and Little brother, trying to make sure he doesn't take out any older people!) Recently he took some stickers along with us to the supermarket. While I was busy trying to pack quicker than the shopping, which was coming down the belt at speed, he made it his mission to give every person he could find a sticker. I'm trying to teach him practical skills and he's teaching me generosity and kindness in moments where I might otherwise choose to be stressed.

I don't want to burden my kids unnecessarily with some of the challenges we're facing but there are ways in which we can involve them age-appropriately, for example talking about whether we can afford something this month and inviting them to help choose what not to buy in order to save for something else. Big brother also helps to unpack the shopping when we get home and loves taking an active part in helping to get our meals ready in the week.

I talk to my son about budgeting and putting money aside for special occasions and I let him learn from his own errors (providing it's not too dangerous!). For example, if he forgets that he has put a cake in the oven – I prompt him once and then it's over to him. **Marina**

· · · · · · ·

I get my kids to choose one easy meal from a recipe book each week to cook for the family. I busy myself in the kitchen in the background in case of emergency, but, as far as possible, I try to let them do as much as they can. It gives them a great sense of achievement and has the added benefit of my picky eater eating food he might otherwise refuse to eat if I had made it! **Kat**

· · · · · · ·

A piece of advice that I read was to ask your kid if they needed help with a specific part of a challenge rather than the whole thing, so that they learn to identify which bit they are struggling with. If my daughter says she needs help with her shoe, I get her to be more specific. Is it getting the shoe on? Getting it on the correct foot? The laces? I've found this is helping her grow in confidence (and it helps me to not be too controlling and take over!). **Emma-Louise**

· · · · · · ·

We encouraged our kids to do things like washing their own clothes, stacking the dishwasher, washing up, ironing their own clothes and making meals occasionally. Now that my son is 17 years old, he is also able to do things like learning to drive and helping to cook food on the BBQ. When possible, they are also given opportunities to serve at church. **Carol**

If children only hear the message that they are special, that they are amazing, that they can do anything and that they can be anything they want, what happens when those statements get challenged? What happens when our kids fail an exam? Or when they go to work for the first time and have a hard time keeping up with their colleagues? Or when they get rejected in some way?

I want my kids to be bold and confident and to ambitiously chase their dreams, but I don't want them to leave home thinking they are the most special person in the world and can do absolutely anything they want. Life throws up disappointments and challenges and I don't want them to be shocked when these come in their way. My hope is that they will be realistic and ready to take on those challenges with an unshakeable confidence, which comes from God.

When I think about confidence, I think about Moses. When God called Moses to go and rescue His people, Moses had a crisis of confidence. He said he couldn't do it. But God didn't say, 'You're amazing, you've got this. Be confident in who you are.' He said exactly what Moses needed to know, 'I will be with you' (Exod. 3:12).

And in Joshua 1:9, God didn't simply say to Joshua, 'Be strong and courageous'. He said, 'Be strong and courageous... *for* the LORD your God will be with you wherever you go' (added emphasis).

I want my kids to know they can be confident *because* God is with them. I want them to know that God loves them immensely, wants to spend time with them and invites them to be part of His plans. In *Parenting Children for a Life of Faith*[3], Rachel Turner gives an excellent framework for rethinking how to help your kids build a core of confidence, which has really helped me to think about how I do this with my kids in times of success as well as in times of failure.

In one of my previous jobs, the manager would get everyone to share their biggest fails and successes of the week. Both were viewed as equally valuable and as opportunities to learn. I found myself seeing failure as an incredible opportunity, and a normal part of everyday life. Each time I failed, I was grateful that I had stepped out of my comfort zone and created an experience I could learn from.

As parents, we will get lots of opportunities to coach our kids through times of failure: when they fail a test, if they struggle to make a friend or when they try to make a craft and it doesn't look how they wanted it to.

How we react and talk about failure can be powerful. How we help our kids learn and grow through it, and how we show them that we're not disappointed in them, or ourselves, can be huge in helping them learn to cope with their own failures in the future.

It's also incredibly powerful when we share our own failure stories in conversation with them, like when I told Big brother how I upset my friend because I said something that wasn't thoughtful, and explained how I fixed it by saying sorry and chatting with my friend. When we share what we've learnt through failure, we give them permission to do the same. We help them to learn that when they fail, they can brush themselves off and get back up again knowing that failing is normal but they are not a failure.

I think it's important that little ones know that everyone gets things wrong sometimes and that it's important to be able to say sorry. **Iva**

Preparing my children for life and the world doesn't mean that I'm wishing away my time with them. I love them and do all I can to protect them, but I also endeavour to always help them to learn and grow from their experiences. I talk about what choices they have. I ask them, 'What can I do? What would make you feel better?' I help to give them power in their pain to figure out how they would like to choose to respond. Rather than telling them what to do or telling them not to cry, I try to help them in that moment. I'm doing all I can to prepare them for the world, to try to equip them to be able to handle anything that comes their way without me by their side.

Both my boys have shown themselves to have an independent and rather stubborn streak. Big brother, in particular, has always liked to do things for himself (until he gets cross and then I must do it for him – immediately!). I love it when he wants to do things on his own, but if I'm honest, I also really love it when he shows me that he still needs me too. If I arrive to pick him up from somewhere and he spots me and shouts, 'Mummy!' as he attaches himself to my leg like a little limpet, it makes my heart happy – particularly as all I usually get is a quick glance before he goes back to playing.

As parents, we might say that we don't feel our kids are ready for things, or that they're growing up too quickly, but perhaps that says more about us than them. Perhaps it's us that need the affirmation of their need of us. When it comes to letting go of our kids, we need to prepare ourselves to let go as much as we need to prepare them – if not more. It's up to us to choose to trust them to make their own decisions. It's up to us to choose what kind of in-laws we'll be if our kids get married. And it's up to us to choose how we'll love and support them when they no longer live under our roof. And again, while we don't want to wish our time away, it might be wise to prepare ourselves before it happens.

Pete says...

I've found it trickier to let go of the boys, or at least our eldest. I've had to learn how to widen my boundaries of control and safety in order for him to develop, learn and grow. Whenever our family goes to a soft play area or the park, I'm astonished at the difference between Annie and myself. As Annie spends a lot more time with the boys, she certainly knows their capabilities far better than I do but she also encourages the boys to explore far more than I do. At first, I was a hovering dad, waiting to catch them from every possible fall and stumble they might face. To some extent, I'm still that dad, however, I'm learning to let go a little. Our eldest will hopefully be riding a bike soon (without stabilisers) and swimming. They are growing up and I won't always be there to catch them.

While still enjoying the present, perhaps there are ways we can prepare ourselves now for when they go to secondary school, or move out or get married, and the role of mum begins to look a bit different. Some parents may feel bereft when their kids leave. I chatted to my mum about what it was like when my brother and I left home and I hadn't anticipated that she would still feel pressure, from other parents, to respond a certain way.

My mum said she felt prepared to let us go and her overriding feeling was excitement for the opportunities that were in store for us. However, she received a lot of comments that her reaction wasn't normal and that the empty nest syndrome would hit her eventually. More than ten years on, it hasn't yet!

I've had enough conversations now with friends to know that whatever your situation, the blending of families is not always easy; it's not uncommon to have a difficult relationship with your parents-in-law.

Since becoming a mum, I have started to think about what kind of mother-in-law I will be. I have seen my mum be a mother-in-law to my husband and to my sister-in-law, and I have a mother-in-law, so I've already learnt a bit about what I want to do – and not do. In particular, I know how much I have valued my parents' constant love and support over the years and how they've always been ready to help without judgment. I don't want to assume that my future relationships with children-in-law will be difficult. I want to consciously do all I can to make them as good as they can possibly be.

My mother-in-law has struggled to accept me as part of the family. She has been very controlling and liked to dictate when and how we did things. She has said some very hurtful things over the years and I have just had to quietly sit and accept them, so as

*not to upset my husband. But the worse thing has
been the silent control she has over my husband. His
life has been ruled by a sense of 'I can't do that, my
mother wouldn't like it,' or 'My mother might ask me
to do this.' A lot of the time it has been very tough
but I just have to remind myself that I was chosen by
my husband and I am important in his life.*
Anonymous

It's not easy to marry into a family when your mother-
in-law is unwilling to accept you. This can be particularly
difficult when she still has some kind of control over
her child. Letting go of your child and seeing them as
someone else's spouse, particularly when you don't
approve of them, is a challenge. Let's remember that,
when we reach that stage in life, we have the power to
choose to let go well. We can choose to love our child's
partner and welcome them. We can choose to let go of
needing to have control in our child's life and trust them
to make decisions and start their own family. I don't deny
that this might be difficult but I want to be prepared, so
that I do everything I can to make the relationships I
have with my future children-in-law a positive one. To
be honest, I don't know how best to prepare myself for
letting my kids go, but I do know that I want to try.

My parents allowed me to become an independent adult
while also always being there when I needed them. Pete and
I are trying to do the same: give our kids more freedom and
encourage them to make their own choices while always
letting them know we're here for them. We also practice
loving and welcoming other kids into our home regularly,

making our home an open space for them to bring others in.

As well as preparing myself to be a good mother-in-law, I also hope to one day be a grandmother or even great-grandmother who loves and supports my children and grandchildren through prayer.

As grandparents and now great-grandparents, we were able to bring these busy people to our great God in prayer on a daily basis. We pray that God will give us the wisdom to continue to encourage them all to know that they are each made in His image and that He has love and purposes for them. **Margaret**

Margaret's prayer is my prayer too: that God would give me wisdom to continue to encourage my kids to be who He has created them to be, and that He would give me a willingness to let them be who He is calling them to be.

As you become an older mum (I am 72), your relationships with your children have to adapt to accept the changes in their lives. We no longer decide what they can and can't do and neither should we, even if we really wish we could! If they go away to university or a year out, this is a big change for them and for me and my husband. You adapt to the empty bedroom and the long chats late at night, but the absence of the jokes and noise and various musical instruments is a reminder that they are making their own way into the world and don't need Blue Ted anymore! (Blue Ted is a teddy bought for my now 44-year-old son the day he was born and still resides with him – albeit pretty battered!)

I found it testing, yet sort of wonderful to let go when my oldest son married. Overnight you become both mum and mother-in-law! I still remember the mix of anxiety and sorrow when I realised that I wasn't the most important woman in my son's life anymore. But I accept that this is the only way it should be. My daughter-in-law is a strong-minded Christian and a lovely woman. However, we are very different and it takes time and determination to really get to know one another and to develop a loving understanding for each other. The inevitable clashes occur from time to time, but because we have worked at respecting each other's viewpoints, we talk through these difficulties when they arise and put things right as soon as we can. I actually believe that we are getting closer through these difficult times. I love those moments when we can have 'girly' chats that blokes wouldn't even begin to understand, or would cause them to blush. Sometimes we do it on purpose just for the sheer naughtiness of it!

My son and his wife now have three children, so I have become a grandma! Being with young energetic children is a joy and another challenge as you get older because our ageing bodies remind us that we can't throw them up in the air and climb trees as easily as we used to – although there is no harm in making them laugh when you try!

I now see my sons as sensitive, intelligent,

sometimes annoying, individual, fun and caring adults. We talk for ages about what the grandchildren are up to and how life is changing as we all get older.

If I could offer any wisdom in setting your children free to be all God designed them to be, it is this: keep talking together, make time to see each other (even when you are not being asked to babysit) and tell them often how much you love them, and always be free with hugs. They still need them and so do we. **Mary**

THINKING HONESTLY

What conversation can you choose to have with your kid this week that takes a step towards more open and honest conversations for you as a family?

What are you doing to help prepare your kids for the world?

What are you doing to help prepare yourself for letting go of your kids?

[1]S. McManus, P. Bebbington, R. Jenkins and T. Brugha (Eds.), 'Mental health and wellbeing in England: Adult Psychiatric Morbidity Survey 2014', taken from digital.nhs.uk [Accessed October 2019]
[2]Walt Disney Studios, 2016
[3]Rachel Turner, *Parenting Children for a Life of Faith* – Omnibus Edition (Oxford: BRF, 2018)

10

Ways a friend makes a good mum friend

Work friends, church friends, old friends, new friends – we all have a range of friends. Here are some of the unique qualities that make a good mum friend.

1 She doesn't judge you. In fact, she doesn't even notice whether you've done your hair, got baby sick on your clothes, or if you let your kids watch TV all afternoon, because she probably has too.

2 She understands the incomprehensible messages you sent while trying to wrestle your toddler away from your phone.

3 Your kids become interchangeable, eating regularly at each other's homes.

4 She can pick up on a conversation whether it was interrupted an hour, a week or a month ago.

5 She tells you when you're doing a good job, particularly when you feel like you're not.

6 If you say you're knackered and just need some time on your own she understands and forgives you for cancelling at the last minute. Equally she still wants to hang out even if you're knackered and don't feel like you're very good company.

7 If you head to hers in the evening wearing your pyjamas and carrying a bottle of wine, you know she'll open the door in her pyjamas too.

8 She doesn't do kid comparison (apart from to reassure you that your kids are as normal, or at least as weird, as hers!).

9 You don't need to tidy up before she comes round.

10 She brings supplies when she visits – cake, coffee, microwave dinners for the kids, wine or gin – whatever works for you both!

We probably won't find someone who ticks every box on this list (if you do, hold her tight and never let her go!) but these are definitely some qualities that make for good mum friendships.

Supportive community

When the poo soaks through every layer of clothing, who's got your back? I expect you thought that this far into the book you were done with the poo stories. Apologies. But are we ever really done with the poo in parenthood? It's the reality of being a parent. There will be poo, and there will be vomit. It will get everywhere. And we will be the ones who have to clean it up.

When Big brother was younger, I remember one particularly messy day. I arrived at church and went to lift him out of his buggy and as I leant over him, I smelt that smell. You know the one. The smell of a dirty nappy that is so much worse than normal. The smell that tells you the poo is no longer all contained inside the nappy. I picked him up, grabbed the changing bag, and power-walked (holding him at arm's length) to a little room at the back of church where I could change him.

As I was stripping away *all* his clothes and using a billion wipes, I realised I didn't have a spare change of clothes with me. I *always* had spare clothes but obviously not on the one day I desperately needed them.

So I got on the phone (while holding down my wriggly, poo-covered toddler) to call my brother and sister-in-law who had been at my house and were meeting me at church, but they'd already left. I started calling other mum friends I knew would be coming to church who might have clothes with them. But to no avail.

Poo clothes bagged up, I set my toddler (clothed only in a nappy) loose and wondered what I should do. Big brother was more than happy to run around in church in just a nappy – he'd like to live his entire life that way, I'm sure.

Fortunately, I spotted another mum friend and managed to borrow some clothing. My brother and another friend also called back to offer to go buy clothing. The support to help clothe my naked little guy was overwhelming.

Of course, less than an hour later, the little guy did another poo that went through his borrowed clothes! Another mum changed his nappy – that's real community. This time we bought a new outfit as we were off out to lunch and didn't much fancy the lingering poo smell while we ate! Although, obviously, we did leave him asleep in them for an hour first. In the list of baby and toddler priorities, sleep trumps poo, right?

At the time this happened, we'd only been at our church for six months, having not known anyone before we arrived. It made me realise that we had joined an incredible community where I already had friends who felt like family.

Motherhood is so much easier when we do it together, side-by-side; when we have people who are there for us in the good times and in the inevitable messy moments of motherhood.

Friendships change in parenthood. We might find we no longer see the friends we used to see every day at work.

Perhaps we now go to a different church service, or we just struggle to see people as much as we used to now that our circumstances have changed. When everything else is shifting, it can feel all the more unsettling when our relationships are changing too.

Finding a caring community is probably the best way to handle most of the challenges of parenthood. Parenting in community is easier. It's lighter. It's less lonely. But, finding the right community isn't always easy. As someone who is naturally introverted and has found making deep friendships difficult, I get that it isn't easy. However, I can look back and know that it has always been worth choosing to step out of my comfort zone to seek community.

When I was 11 years old, another girl convinced my 'best friend' to un-invite me from her ice-skating and bowling birthday party. After lots of tears, sitting on my own in the playground, and probably some words between parents, I was re-invited. I can still remember the pain of the rejection. I also vividly remember the concussion and whiplash I got falling during my first experience ice-skating. All in all, a pretty unforgettable time.

I have always found making friends quite difficult. Growing up, I tended to be friends with everyone but not anyone's best friend. And if I did ever have a 'best friend', it felt like it wasn't long before someone new and more interesting came along and shunted me out of the position. I was often bullied as a kid and it's taken me a long time to learn to be resilient and to not care what other people think. Most of the time.

Parenthood can sometimes feel incredibly lonely. I honestly don't know how I'd get through motherhood without my friendships and community. Choosing to be vulnerable and intentional in friendship has been so worthwhile but it's not always been easy or without its challenges. As a parent, some days I feel like all I hear is my own voice. I've been to baby and toddler groups, surrounded by people I'd like chat to, but have struggled to make eye contact or break into any of the already established groups.

Action for Children did a poll with over 2,000 parents and found that over half had experienced loneliness, with a fifth of those feeling lonely in the last week.[1]

I know lots of people who still have friends from when they were at school together or even younger, but I feel like it's taken me pretty much my whole life, so far, to figure out how to make those sort of lasting friendships. I have found that making close friends as an adult has been both deeply joy-bringing and heart breaking. When we lived in London, I spent a few years building deep friendships and then, in quick succession, most of my close friends left the city. I was devastated. I remember sitting in our church café and sobbing so hard I could hardly speak.

When we moved to Reading, we didn't know anyone and I was faced with the daunting prospect of making new friends again. It wasn't the idea of meeting and chatting to people that I found daunting (I genuinely love that) but instead it was finding those deeper friendships, the friends I can text about random things I find funny or talk to about anything or call 'just because'. The 'best friends'. It was the fear of making and then losing them, or that they might lose interest in me.

This made me quite guarded. I didn't want to give too much of myself away in case they left and I had to go through the whole process again with someone new. But, obviously, this made it impossible to build deep friendships where I felt I could be totally honest and completely myself. I had to make a call as to whether the risk of getting hurt was worth investing in a new friendship.

I remember meeting my friend, Jos, at church on my first morning there and knowing that we would get on well. She and her family seemed pretty settled in Reading, so I felt like the risk was low. A few years later, however, they announced they would be moving away! Thankfully (for me) their circumstances changed again and they stayed, but knowing I had made the choice to invest, in spite of the risk of getting hurt, helped me. It helped me to focus on the friendship I had built rather than the loss or any fear of losing our friendship.

Making that choice wasn't important just for me but for my kids. It's easy to assume that they will just make their own friendships but I know that our boys learn so much from what Pete and I model. I ask myself a lot of questions when it comes to how I'm modelling relationships for them. How well am I equipping them to build friendships? Am I modelling the kind of friendly behaviour that I expect from them? Do I always speak well of my friends? Do I talk to and befriend the people others aren't being friendly towards? Am I brave and do I just go talk to people? It challenges me to go deeper in my relationships and talk with the boys about them. I hope as we learn alongside each other, I can help them to learn to let their guard down and share their hearts, so they can build deep friendships right away, not wait until they're adults.

Making friends will look different for each of us because of where we live, what our local community is like and what our church is like. Like I said, when we moved a few years ago, I chose to be really intentional about trying to make friends. Here are some of the ways that helped me find friends and community.

Getting involved at church

I got stuck in at church where I knew I'd be able to meet people in similar situations. I went along to our weekly women's group (somewhere I probably wouldn't ordinarily have chosen to go). And when someone said, 'Oh, it'd be lovely to have you over sometime,' I'd say, 'I'd love that, can I take your number?' or 'When are you free this week?' I seized opportunities to spend time getting to know people.

Going wider than church

Before we became parents, Pete and I both worked for a church and I felt a little bit stuck inside a Christian bubble. We were working a lot of evenings and our life revolved around church. I didn't really have any friends outside of it. So when I stopped working for a church and we moved to Reading, I was keen to go wider with my friendships.
I joined an app called 'Mummy Social', which is a bit like online dating for mums. A few mums I met, I didn't see again; one mum I really enjoyed hanging out with and then she suddenly stopped messaging me; and then I met my lovely friend, Louisa, and we bonded over the fact that we hardly managed to even talk as we both had incredibly energetic toddlers who liked to run in opposite directions.

Our friendship, and our kids' love for one another, has only grown stronger since.

Another way I have met people locally is through community based social media groups or apps. For example, I found out through Facebook that a road in our neighbourhood was holding a 'play street' where they closed off the road and invited kids to come play. It was a great way to meet a few neighbours and I'm looking forward to going to the next one.

We also have the privilege of having brilliant neighbours. Our kids and theirs pop over the wall into each other's garden to play, and we have literally borrowed sugar from one another. On more than one occasion, Emma, my neighbour, has also made me cups of tea and passed them over the wall in the garden when I've been having a particularly stressful day.

Intentionally creating local community

Our church draws up meal rotas for parents who have just had babies, and I signed up to provide a meal for a mum that I hadn't chatted to before. When I went to drop off the meal, I discovered that she lived only a few minutes' walk from my house. Since then we've spent a lot of time together and we've created a WhatsApp group with other local mums from church and have started to meet up more often.

On a day when I've got nothing planned, I can message the group and see who's free to get together. We've also been able to support each other in all sorts of ways, from using each other's washing machines when ours have broken, to taking each other's kids when we've been ill. Not only that, the dads are now also meeting regularly too.

Pete says...

A couple of us dads were challenged by this community group of mums, and decided to do something similar for the dads and other men in our local area. It's only happened a couple of times but we've really enjoyed hanging out together and getting to know one another better. It's made us re-evaluate how we do small groups at our church, as meeting together as parents on a regular basis doesn't always work (one parent is usually babysitting). The separation of guys and girls, however, has been wonderful, as I've found it's led to much deeper conversations more quickly than might be possible if all couples were there and present together. We hope to then come together with all the families to celebrate, cheer each other on and spend time loving one another.

Finding a supportive community might not always be local but parenting has become easier knowing that we have so many people living nearby who are always up for a chat or ready to help in a crisis. That kind of community is worth seeking out.

Inviting people over in spite of rejection

Being rejected is hard, especially if you've been rejected in previous relationships. In the early days of parenthood, being so tired made me feel even more vulnerable and nervous about trying to make friends. However, if you can choose to focus on the bigger goal of building deeper friendships, and not see rejection as a slight against you, the rewards are huge.

Last Christmas, I invited friends round one evening and as I sat feeding Little brother, my phone kept buzzing as one after another every friend cancelled – it was pretty hard not to feel like it was me. But I know there have been many times when I've planned to go out but struggled to find a babysitter or my kid was sick or after putting my kids to bed, all I've wanted to do is curl up in bed and do nothing.

When you're hanging out with other mums, your social lives are now based around little, unpredictable people and unfortunately that means last minute cancellations are to be expected.

Not compromising

Just because you've always known each other, happen to be part of the same community or seem to have lots in common, you don't have to be friends with someone. Be kind to yourself. People don't get to gain our friendship because of obligation. If someone doesn't respect you or isn't kind, then it's OK to choose to protect yourself by backing away. You and your family come first.

If I'm spending a lot of time with someone who isn't very nice to me and I'm struggling to say anything kind about them at home, or if I'm coming away from seeing them feeling bad about myself, what am I teaching my kids about valuing myself? Also if their child isn't very nice to mine and they come away feeling hurt every time we see them, what am I teaching my kid about relationships? Am I letting him know he can choose not to spend time with someone who makes him feel bad or am I inadvertently teaching him to remain in friendships where he gets hurt?

This all sounds incredibly easy written down – I know it isn't. It's not an easy conversation to have. I once switched my working week around in order to make it more difficult to see someone because their kid was always so unkind to mine, rather than actually having a conversation with the other person about it. I'm not suggesting you suddenly start culling friendships or telling people you won't be seeing them anymore. I didn't do that. However, when I chose to invest more in the friendships that made me feel loved, supported and challenged in a good way, I found so much more life and closeness in my friendships.

Using social media

I have made some amazing mum connections on social media, and I have loved the interaction and connection it brings. In the early days of parenthood, I found I was able to connect with people in the middle of night when feeding, or when I was hiding in the loo. I've decided that while social media helps me build genuine connection and makes me feel encouraged, I will continue to use it, but if that ceases to be the case then I know I need to make a call about using it differently, or not at all.

Having honest and vulnerable friendships

Friendships change and people move away but choosing to invest deeply in friendships can bring so much richness to our relationships. At the start of this book, I shared the conversation I had with a friend where we were both honest and vulnerable with each other. Those are the friendships I want. C.S. Lewis puts it beautifully in *The Four Loves*[2] when he says, 'Friendship is born at that moment when one person says to another, "What! You too? I thought I was the only one."'

Finding community with older people

If I ever buy a magazine, I'll always go for the ones that are full of tips on how to look after your home and garden and how to make recipes when entertaining people. I've been teased about this before by friends but I'd far rather read advice from women 30 years older than me, reflecting on what they've learnt in life, than from women my age or younger.

It's the same with my real-life relationships. While I want to find friends who are in similar situations to me, I also crave community with people who are a different age and stage to me. At church, I've always headed to the service with the biggest range of ages; I've joined life groups with both retired people and young married couples; and at university, I opted to get stuck into church rather than Christian Union so that I could get to know families.

Recently I went to a mother and baby group at a local nursing home and spent some lovely mornings chatting to an older lady who had been very lonely. She definitely wasn't the only one who benefitted from our interaction.

At church, I've begun to seek out friendships with older people. Little brother and I recently spent the morning with a couple in their nineties, hearing about their lives, how they raised their kids and how they viewed church. I left their company feeling enriched, challenged, encouraged and happier.

Unless I intentionally create those relationships, my kids probably wouldn't spend much quality time with people over sixty. I want my boys to learn to interact confidently with people of any age, and I want to seize any opportunity I can to learn from people who are older, wiser and have just lived far more life than me.

The challenges of parenting never really go away, they are just different, but children and grandchildren are a gift from the Lord! There were obviously challenges even in Jesus' earthly family! **Sue**

In the Bible, we see multigenerational community in action over and over again, from the Israelites worshipping together to whole towns and villages coming together to listen to Jesus. Being plugged into a supportive community is important. And Jesus knew that.

Jesus called His disciples to come and be His community. They stuck with Him, they supported Him, they did life with Him. But Jesus' community wasn't just His friends, it was much wider than that. People opened their homes for Him to stay, they fed Him, they washed His feet, a man offered his tomb for Jesus' body and crowds of people came out to welcome Him as He arrived in their towns. Jesus had community with children and adults. He would have stayed with families and we know that He welcomed little children to Him: 'Let the little children come to me, and do not hinder them, for the kingdom of God belongs to such as these' (Mark 10:14).

Loneliness affects us all whether we're parents of a tiny newborn or grandparents whose kids left home years ago. I've been blessed by my mum friends who are experiencing the same challenges and just totally 'get it' and I've also been incredibly encouraged by my older friends who have shared stories, encouraged me and prayed for me where I'm at.

Whether it's with other mums, neighbours or older people, there is so much joy in building diverse community. When we share meals and stories, when we are willing to share our hearts as well as our stuff, we can build deep, loving friendships. We can walk alongside others sharing our pains and our joys, and growing together.

In his letter to the church in Rome, Paul describes what a community should look like: a people who 'love deeply', who are 'inventive in hospitality' and who make 'friends with nobodies' (Rom. 12:10,13,16, *The Message*). That's the kind of community I want to be a part of! And if you are yet to find those special friends, I pray for boldness and confidence for you to step out in vulnerability. I pray for all of us that we would continually find deeper, real connection every day.

THINKING HONESTLY

Who's got your back on the messiest days of parenthood?

Are there other parents you could support when they are in need?

Is there anyone you would like to get to know better? Could you spend time with them this week?

[1]'It starts with hello – A report looking into the impact of loneliness in children, young people and families.' Posted November 2017, taken from actionforchildren.org.uk [Accessed October 2019] p3. Action for Children Parenting Poll, conducted by Survation. Survation interviewed 2,087 parents aged 18+ online from 8–15 September 2017. Survation is a member of the British Polling Council and abides by its rules.
[2]The Four Loves by C.S. Lewis ©copyright C.S. Lewis Pte Ltd 1960.

10

Things I learnt from my granny

When I am older, I would like to be a grandparent like my granny. I am so often aware of her absence, even more acutely at present as I know she would have adored her great-grandsons. I hope the way I live my life now is influenced by how much I learnt from her. She prayed unceasingly; it was her immediate response to go to God and chat to Him. Here are just ten of the many, many things I learnt from my granny.

1 Christmas isn't Christmas without crackers and the *Radio Times* in a hessian shopping bag.

2 If your granddaughter is going to be driving a long journey in the rain, staying up all night to pray for her is no big deal.

3 Pulling faces at your grandkids while Grandpa says grace is great fun.

4 It's important to be able to make a cake in the time it takes your grandchildren to travel to your house.

5 It's important to get involved in church, even if just serving refreshments in the kids' group – every role is important.

6 Glove compartments and bedside tables should always be full of sweets.

7 Use-by dates do not matter, and your grandkids will enjoy playing 'Find the oldest thing in the kitchen'.

8 If you have to use a magnifying glass to see the keypad on your phone then texting might not be for you.

9 Life is for looking after the birds in the garden and loving your family.

10 There's always time for a cup of tea.

I have so many memories of my granny. I wonder if, one day in the future, my grandchildren will reflect on what they have learnt from me. Will they remember me as a prayerful, faithful, fun granny? I hope at least to have taught them some of the things that my granny taught me.

Marriage and the night with the bread

During my first pregnancy, I felt nauseous all day every day apart from two weeks in the middle. This meant I found it really hard to cook as the smell of food would turn my stomach, even going to a supermarket was a challenge.

One particularly rough evening, while Pete was at work, I thought I might just be able to manage some toast with butter. Unfortunately we'd run out of bread, so I sent a desperate text to Pete, asking him to bring some home, then I snuggled up in bed and waited for my bread.

When he returned home empty handed, I don't know what came over me. Actually, I do. Hormones. I burst into tears and became totally inconsolable. It was ugly. I was possibly the most upset I've ever been. And it was completely irrational.

I've never seen Pete move so quickly as he retreated back out the door to buy the bread. He couldn't drive at that point, so he was forced to run to the shops. Unfortunately I was on a gluten-free diet at the time, and gluten-free bread wasn't easy to come by in our local shops. He ran to the Co-op. No bread. Then on to

Waitrose. No bread.

I can't imagine how Pete must have felt jogging back to his completely irrational, ugly-crying wife. I tried to hold myself together, and I'd love to tell you that I graciously accepted that he'd done all he could and that I would be OK without the bread, but, in fact, I cried myself to sleep. And I mean big, dramatic, can't calm yourself down sobs. It was pretty hideous.

Pete says...

I could comment more but perhaps all I'll say is this: that was a difficult night. Partly because of the emotion and hormones, and partly because I'd never needed to run so far and fast in my life!

Things weren't much better during my second pregnancy. After a particularly enthusiastic rant about how Pete wasn't cleaning the oven the way I wanted him to, Pete looked at my bump and said, 'I think maybe we won't do pregnancy again.'

Becoming parents is a huge shift in our relationship with our partner. Suddenly we have another little person to think about. Another person who is pretty keen to take a whole lot of our attention, time and sleep. Being intimate and connecting with one another can become the last thing on our minds when we've only had two hours sleep, our clothes no longer fit and when it feels all our attention is being taken up by the baby permanently attached to us.

'"the two will become one flesh." So they are no longer two, but one flesh. Therefore what God has joined together, let no one separate.' Mark 10:8–9

When we get married we choose to become a team. Preparing to add another person to the team can be a really special and exciting time; we know it won't be just the two of us for much longer. But more than that, we have an opportunity to prepare ourselves as a couple spiritually and emotionally to be the best team we can be before welcoming a child into our family. Just like in the early days of being a couple, it's good to be really intentional about loving each other well and strengthening our team. It doesn't just happen.

Pete and I could have totally blamed the night with the bread on hormones and tried to forget about it. Instead we chose to talk about it. By talking together, Pete shared why he'd forgotten the bread, and I was able to share how I wasn't feeling very 'remembered' or heard very often. As we dug deeper, we realised that the stress he was experiencing at work was having a huge impact on how well he was able to retain information and listen. We had to figure out how to communicate better, in spite of the hormones and stress. We agreed to regularly ask how each other was feeling, and that it was OK for me to prompt him by asking 'How are you going to remember? Shall we pop a reminder on the calendar?' Three years on and we're still in that habit.

Becoming a couple, getting married, getting pregnant and then actually having children meant our circumstances regularly shifted, and we found it was almost like we needed to learn again, or at least be really intentional about continuing to work on our marriage. So how can we be intentional about strengthening our marriages? Firstly, let me shatter the illusion that Pete and I have got it figured out when it comes to communication. I think we will be learning how to communicate better for the rest of our lives. Some days we're great at communication, some days we fail miserably but what matters is that we're working on it.

One of the wonderful things about communication is that it's possible to have different approaches. We first thought about how we communicated during a marriage preparation course, and realised that we come from families who process things very differently – and our life experiences have led to us learning different ways of talking through things and responding to emotion and conflict. Through sharing and learning from experience, we have found ways to try to communicate better together. For example when something big happens, Pete usually likes at least three weeks to think about it before discussing the implications with me, whereas I like to talk about things immediately. So we've had to agree that I will wait a short time but also that he will be willing to talk sooner. We've also learnt that we naturally communicate better at opposite times of day to each other: I like to talk last thing at night, where as Pete likes to chat during the day. We've had to find times to talk that works for both of us.

I've lost count of the number of times when I've sat stewing, thinking that Pete has done something to upset me intentionally and he's been blissfully unaware that he's caused me any offence. Post-baby, Pete assumed that I wanted space and was choosing to sit the other end of the sofa from me, when actually all I wanted was to be close to him. Eventually I decided to be honest about how I was feeling and it was resolved. Being honest and sharing what we're feeling is such an easy solution but how often do we sit and stew instead?

As first-time parents, Pete and I would regularly play board games after our son had gone to bed. Second time around, with a toddler and baby, we've found we're often pretty tired but that we really value just being together, so we'll find a TV series to watch together. Even if we're falling asleep, we find connection just by choosing to be together in the same space sharing an experience.

Some friends of ours once told us about how they do a marriage MOT every six months when they reflect on their last six months and they create a vision for the next six months of their marriage. Pete and I do something similar annually on our anniversary when we ask each other about the year gone by and talk about what we'd like to do differently and achieve in the year ahead.

In the chapter about connecting with our kids, I mentioned the concept of different love languages: words of affirmation, quality time, receiving gifts, acts of service and physical touch. When you know each other's love language, then it can really help you to show each other love more effectively. Even if you have already explored this idea as a couple, it's definitely worth revisiting as sometimes your love language changes, particularly after having kids.

Connecting with God can look really different as our

circumstances change. Pete and I have been through phases of doing devotionals and journalling together, listening to worship songs together, and trying to create space to pray together. Become parents has changed the rhythm of our lives, and often we'll suddenly realise that three weeks have gone by and we've not had any devotional time together, so we'll either try again or we'll find new ways of connecting with God as a couple.

When it's 4am and you haven't got to sleep yet but your partner is snoring peacefully beside you, or when you're handed a screaming baby as soon as you walk through the door after a long day at work, it can be pretty difficult to be patient and feel connected with one another. Our partners see the very best – and the very worst – of us. But that's what we're committed to. Life. In all its messiness.

If you're moving into another phase of parenthood, it's a good idea to talk about what your roles will be beforehand; for example, if you're expecting a baby, will you both be prepared to change the nappies? Will you be breastfeeding only or adding in bottles for your partner to do? What will the nights look like? Talking about your expectations can help you get excited, help to alleviate any worries, and also highlight where you might be expecting different things.

Being on the same page as Pete really helped to unite us, particularly when the opinions of everyone else came our way as we were confident in what we were doing. When both partners are intentional about strengthening their relationship, it helps to create a strong team able to face all the highs and lows that parenthood brings. Paul's advice to the church in Ephesus on how to relate to one another is great advice for couples, friends and family members; it's the gold standard for all relationships.

> 'Be completely humble and gentle; be patient, bearing with one another in love. Make every effort to keep the unity of the Spirit through the bond of peace.' Ephesians 4:2–3

I don't know whether I will ever reach complete humility and gentleness, but I think that bearing with one another in love sums up how we can feel in parenthood: reminding ourselves of our love for each other, and asking God to remind us of His love particularly helps on our most tired days. I also love how Paul says to 'make every effort to keep the unity of the Spirit through the bond of peace'. Paul knows it's not easy but he urges us to try to be united and peaceful in all of our relationships.

THINKING HONESTLY

How can you continue spending time with your partner when you're both tired and fitting in a new schedule around a baby?

Have you ever figured out your love languages, or those of your partner? If you haven't, why not take time to discuss what they could be as a couple?

What could you do today to gain a deeper connection with your partner?

10

Ways to keep the romance alive

Keeping the romance alive in your marriage once kids come along can be pretty tricky, particularly if you were never particularly romantic in the first place! Here are ten easy things you can do to add a little spark to your relationship.

1 You know how in films they dramatically sweep things off a table to get 'intimate'? Well you can do this too, with all the laundry on the bed. You're only going to put it on the floor at night-time anyway, so why not romantically use it to your advantage.

2 Talk about your days. Nothing says 'I love you' more than actually being listened to when you explain how the highlight of your day was that you pulled all the hair out of the hoover or cleaned the bird poo off the garden toys.

3 Share a secret code. Spell things out just for one another – just watch out when your kids start learning to spell.

4 Hold hands. It's really nice, even just for a moment, to hold a hand that's not dirty, sticky or constantly squirming to get away.

5 Buy each other cards – and give them. Pete carried my anniversary card in his bag, unwritten, for months after our anniversary. It's the thought that counts, right?

6 Let them have more of the duvet. Maybe... Just for a night...

7 If you're watching a TV series together and you sneak an episode in on your own, or hear a spoiler, act as if it's the first time you've seen it when you eventually watch it together.

8 Act surprised, or at least fully interested, when they retell you a story for the third time because they're so flipping tired they can't remember who they've told.

9 Tackle a house or garden job together to spend some time bonding; particularly romantic tasks include sorting the under the stairs cupboard, getting things down from the loft and any kind of car maintenance.

10 Dates are different now but you can still go out for dinner. There's nothing quite like staring lovingly into each other's eyes while one child spills juice on your lap and the other climbs on the table.

Obviously, these ideas are all a little bit of fun but sometimes, as couples, it can be easy to forget that we are two people who have chosen to be together rather than two people who parenting alongside each other in the midst of the everyday busyness. What could you do to remind one another that you are still those two people who fell in love?

Connecting with God

I couldn't imagine doing life without God. In fact, I couldn't imagine doing parenthood without God. But it's difficult to find time to connect with God with crying children, constant requests for snacks, overwhelming tiredness (us and them) and all the other things we end up juggling in parenthood.

When Big brother was born, it was an incredible spiritual experience for me. It might have been partly down to the effects of the gas and air but I've never felt closer to God or spent so much time chatting to Him. In the birthing pool, I felt that it was only me and God in the room. I sensed His presence so tangibly, and even in moments of intense pain, I felt connected to Him.

When Big brother finally arrived, he came out with the cord and his arm around his neck (like a little Superman), and he had to be whisked away to be resuscitated. I remember lying there, collapsed on the bed, legs akimbo, being stitched up yet fully focusing on trusting God and waiting for my baby to come back, so I could meet him; not how I imagined I might one day describe my best 'God moment'.

Meanwhile the doctors resuscitated him outside the room and asked Pete to come and 'connect with him'.

Pete did what he'd been doing throughout my pregnancy and he sung over our baby boy. As our son arrived into the world, I felt acutely aware of the fragility of life. In that moment, I couldn't have imagined going on the journey of parenthood without God, and it's been the same every day since.

Before I became a mum, a friend told me that those first few years as a new mum were her most difficult but also her most joy-filled, in terms of her faith. While she still had big unanswered questions and, at times, felt disconnected from Him, she'd never known God's love more or been so in awe of Him. At the time, I had no idea how that could feel. Now, I get it. The highs and lows can feel extreme. Some days, I might only manage whispered, desperate prayers, or get to the end of the day and realise that I hadn't chatted to God at all. Other days, Big brother asks me a profound question and I spend all day marvelling at the God who created us and gave my kid the ability to ask such deep questions with a feather-like lightness.

As a parent, my faith has become completely interwoven into the messiness of everyday life. I'm on a constant journey in my relationship with God, daily figuring out how to connect with Him in each season and learning more about Him and myself. That can be both incredibly exciting and incredibly daunting.

I don't make it to as many prayer meetings at church or listen to as many sermons but I do chat to God while wiping bottoms and snotty noses. I ask Him for strength to face another *very* early wake up. I turn the worship music up loud as the boys crash through the kitchen and get under my feet while I cook; and I cry out to God in the car as I do the nursery run, after hearing bad news from a friend.

Once we enter parenthood, it can be easy to dwell on how much more of a challenge it feels to connect with God. It might feel difficult to get back into our previous rhythms in our relationship with Him or to prioritise even trying to do that. It can feel like doing faith during parenthood is harder. I like to think of it as *different*. Not harder. That shift in language has been hugely important for me.

My relationship with God *has* changed, just like other relationships grow and develop as circumstances and seasons change. This new chapter of life hasn't made my faith in God weaker. In fact, parenthood has enriched my faith and deepened my dependence on God, giving me so much joy. When I shifted my perspective and chose to see life as different, I was able to focus on how I was going to connect with God in this season. If I'd chosen to feel instead like my faith was victim to the adjustment of parenthood and believed that I was simply entering a 'worse' season, I would have been totally missing out.

To be honest, my own faith fell off a cliff when my son was born because I struggled to make it to church, and it's only since starting to make time to go to church and women's group that I have started to feel more connected to it. I think for me, the problem is guilt, so if I'm not doing anything, I feel guilty and do even less to avoid the guilt. To keep a focus on what God is doing and my relationship with Him, I need to be at least semi-engaged in stuff outside of my own life. **Katharine**

Don't feel guilty about the little time you spend with God. As the parenting phases move on, there will be more time. God understands. **Heather**

You'll have learnt by now that I'm pretty passionate about reminding myself that I always have choices and that I can be powerful in making those choices. It's no different when it comes to my faith. For example, my mind wanders now more than ever before, and sometimes I fall asleep in the middle of doing something because I'm so flipping tired. This means that when I actually do get to listen to a sermon at church, I find that I'm not always great at listening. Or when I sit down to spend time with God, I find I wake up suddenly, drool down my face, and realise that I've taken a surprise nap! Choosing to be OK with that has been transformational for me. It's easy to feel guilty about our inability to spend much time with God. But if we choose to ditch the guilt and embrace the difference, then instead of constantly feeling guilty, we free ourselves up to enjoy the time we *do* spend with God instead.

Before I became a mum, I took it for granted that I could sit and read my Bible for hours if I wanted to, or that I could decide last minute to go along to a prayer event at church. Now, it feels like all I get are fleeting moments to spend with God. Where once it was like gulping down a big refreshing drink of water, now I get little sips here and there. It's a bit like becoming flamingoes. If you picture a flamingo, the first thing that comes to mind is probably their colour: beautiful pink plumes. But actually flamingos are *not* pink. They are born with grey feathers but because of the natural dye in the shrimp and algae they eat, their feathers gradually turn pink. Their diet changes what they look like on the outside. Similarly for us, if we want to look like Jesus then we need to spend time with Him, *feeding* on His Word and asking Him to speak to us. If the flamingos ate their shrimp all at once, they would choke; they eat consistently, little and often, taking small sips and eating small snacks.

Spiritual snacking throughout the day helps us to grow more like Jesus. We can read a verse and let it sink deep, asking God to speak to us throughout the day. We can chat to Him in snippets as we do all the little jobs parenthood requires. And the amazing thing is that, even if we only feel we have time for tiny sips, God meets with us and has the power to refresh us abundantly. He wants to spend time with us in relationship. He doesn't say only come to me if you've got a long chunk of time. He says, 'Come to me' (Matt. 11:28). He simply invites us to come to Him.

Even before becoming a parent, I'd discovered the Parenting for Faith course and it made me think differently about how I did my own faith. I loved the idea of chatting to God and 'catching from Him' (how we receive from Him), and I decided that I wanted to chat to God more intentionally throughout the day rather than just in the quieter or planned moments. I began to change the way I communicated with God, choosing to talk with Him honestly and regularly throughout my day and asking Him to speak to me. This became a habit by the time I became a parent and it made such a difference for me.

Expressing my adoration for God as I hold my teething baby and marvel at how God created the pudgy little fingers he's shoving into his dribbly mouth is worship.

Showing up and saying, 'I'm tired but I'm here, God' is worship. It takes another shift in perspective. We don't need to get back into exactly how we used to worship at church. It looks different now and that's OK.

As I've already shared, my church community inspire and challenge me. I meet regularly with a group of mums to pray and they are people with whom I can talk to openly and honestly about the challenges of doing faith in motherhood. They are women who don't judge me when I'm struggling and who celebrate when I've had an answer to prayer. It's so easy to think that everyone else has it sorted but they don't, and just knowing you're not alone in your experience, or in your current season, makes all the difference.

Church can be hard as a parent – if you even manage to get there at all. It can be hard to focus in the service or convince your kid to go to their group. It can feel like everyone is staring at you as you try to drag your screaming kid off the stage, or shush them as they loudly announce they need a poo during the quiet prayer time. Before having kids, being in church may have been the place where we found most connection with God and community, and then, all of a sudden, it becomes a frantic, tiring and even lonely place.

Accepting that church as a parent was going to look different was the first step for me. I was no longer going to be able to chat to all the people I wanted to, or sit quietly reading my Bible during the worship. Rather than disengaging or feeling like it's not possible to connect with God at church anymore, I changed my expectations. I no longer stand alone totally immersed in a set of worship songs but I do get to stand and hold my little one close as I sing during worship. There is actually something incredible about getting to do that in a place of worship. Previously, it might have taken a few songs before I got into an attitude of worship, but now, knowing that any moment I might be called to do a toilet run, I choose to get *in* immediately. I no longer have the luxury of settling myself in, getting a drink, sitting for a bit before I choose to be engaged. Now, I'm in the building and I'm *in*. I take the lead from Big brother who runs to the front of the church immediately. I consciously engage with God however I'm physically and mentally placed. God wants to connect with me and I want to connect with Him.

Once we've accepted that this is a different season in church life, then we get to move into figuring out what it might look like. Perhaps we want to commit to being part of the kids team since our kid isn't going to let us leave anyway. Or perhaps this is a season for us to sit and build community with other mums while we feed our little ones. It will look different for each of us.

At our previous church, we had an area with a screen where parents could sit with their little ones and watch the sermon. I sat there a few times but everyone chatted so loudly that I couldn't focus on the talk. At that time I felt I really needed to listen, so I switched on another TV at the other side of the room and sat there to listen. Other times, I've chatted and caught up with other parents. I've chosen to be honest about what it is that I need. It's OK to do what we need to do in order to meet with God at church and for that to look different from week to week.

Arrow prayers were my lifeline. I was too tired for a 'proper' prayer time most of the time. I also made sure I had praying friends and family around me who could pray on my behalf. My mum was totally my prayer support for the parenting phase of life. I also found listening to worship music (between the nursery rhyme tapes) was so uplifting. Thankfully I haven't got out of that habit now my kids have grown up. **Heather**

· · · · · · ·

I've learnt that what's working for me right now might not in a few weeks or months. I've found that being open to exploring different ideas or ways to find time and space with God and remembering that He is my safe place where I can go and be totally honest has helped me a lot. Even if I feel like I have to be the grown up who's holding it all together in the rest of life, I can always let my guard down and be totally honest with God. **Anna**

Helping our kids to connect with God can feel like a really daunting prospect. We might feel that our relationship with God should be better first, or that we need to have all the answers, or that we don't know where to even begin.

Before I became a parent, I thought a lot about how I would help my children connect with God. Of course, that was before the reality of parenting kicked in. I love the quote, 'Parenting was so much easier when I raised my non-existent children hypothetically.' It's so easy to have plans about how we'll do faith when we become parents. Perhaps we imagine how we'll sit quietly and spend time with God before our little ones wake in the morning, or we picture our families singing worship songs together before bed, or reading the Bible together around the table and creating beautiful, reflective crafts, which our kids will treasure forever.

Then we actually become parents and we're pulling the duvets over our heads desperately hoping for at least a few more minutes sleep. Or our kids are bouncing up and down on their beds, not listening at all, as we tell our incredibly engaging (or so we thought) versions of Bible stories.

We don't always know what's happening in our kid's hearts, we have to trust that by showing them by example what our relationship with God looks like that we're helping them learn to connect with God. For the last couple of years, I have prayed aloud every time we've driven past an ambulance. I've also invited Big brother to pray but usually he says, 'You do it.' Last week, unprompted by me, he saw an ambulance and began to pray aloud and then he invited me to pray.

Helping our children connect with God is another opportunity to practise letting them go. I know I need to trust that God has got my kids. And also to trust that they're totally capable of connecting with Him. In the Old Testament, people needed the high priest to go to God on their behalf. But when Jesus came and died for us, we didn't need that anymore. I want to lead my kids to Jesus and sit with them at His feet, but not as a high priest. I want them to know that they are able to connect with

God no matter how old they are and whether I'm with them or not.

Once, at a soft play area, Big brother wanted to play Mary, Joseph and Jesus. He would be Joseph, Little brother would be Jesus but he needed a Mary, so he invited a random girl to join in and be Mary. He then went on to explain, in vivid and pretty graphic detail, the whole gospel story to her and her granny. These episodes remind me not to underestimate them. I'm having to let go, trust them to God and let them figure out what it looks like to be a Christian in the real world.

When I was pregnant with Big brother, he would leap in the womb whenever Pete led worship and I see that same passion in him now. Similarly, Little brother would wriggle whenever we were praying with lots of people, and he is drawn to people now in a way that is different from his brother. They both connected with God before they were even out of the womb – and they connect with Him now.

Big brother went through a phase of saying, 'That's John's church,' every time we passed any church. We figured out through conversation that 'John' was a friend of ours who goes to our church. This continued for months, and we wondered whether God was calling John to train for church leadership. We told John, who categorically replied that no, he wouldn't be going for ordination. Big brother continued to label every church as 'John's church' and a few months later John told us he had actually decided to get ordained! On another occasion, I was at a mums prayer morning and a friend was crying as we prayed. Big brother (who had seemed to be paying little attention) quietly went to her and hugged her as she wept.

Kids haven't got all of the barriers we may have. They don't yet question things in the cynical way we sometimes do. Big brother hears God and he responds to His prompting without hesitation. I learn so much from him. And I am constantly challenged not to underestimate him or God.

So many times, I assume my kids will want to do something in a certain way or won't understand something yet, and then they completely blow me away with amazing ideas of ways to connect with God that I never would have thought of, or different ways of doing things that help me too. An example that comes to mind is when my three-year-old asked why we sing songs to God and whether He liked it. When I unpacked it a bit she said, 'Well, if it's for God, He should get to choose what He'd like to hear', and now often spends time listening to God before she starts singing. It's really shifted the way I think about worship. **Anna**

Pete says...

When Big brother began being interested in outer space, and things bigger than our world, we only had one book that could be considered a space book, *Indescribable*[1] by Matt Redman and Louie Giglio. We turned each page and he would ask question after question, 'What is that, Daddy? Where

is that, Daddy? Is that the sun? Is that planet Earth?'
I am amazed at his potential to ask infinite (and I
mean infinite) amounts of questions. It helps us both
connect with God as we ask Him: 'God, why did You
make that planet that shape? Which is Your favourite
planet, God?' We spend a lot of time singing songs
of worship, admiring beautiful views and chatting
about the things God has made. But by myself, I
don't ask God nearly as many questions as Big
brother does.

There are many ways that lead me to marvel and
turn back to God. A song that I love has the line:
'Lord Your kindness leads me to repentance, to the
heart of God, Your heart oh God is all I want.'[2] I find
that the more I am reminded of God's kindness to
me and our family, the more I am led to a place of
turning back to Him, and when I turn back to Him,
I rest in His love and grace. Sometimes, either Big
brother or I will begin a sentence by saying, 'God
is kind because...' and we give each other time to
remind ourselves of His kindness and His goodness.
This fun little exercise leads us back to Him and His
love. My hope is that as a father I can help remind
my children of God's kindness and His goodness and
enjoy the privilege of being with them when they
turn to Him again and again.

God also uses my kids to speak to me and to others so
often. On more than one occasion, I've been speaking
publicly to a group of people and one of my boys has

ended up attached to me. Afterwards I've expected criticism or for people to say they found it distracting but instead they told me how it encouraged them, or how God spoke to them about God's love for us as His children as they watched my interaction with my kid. We can worry that our kids disturb others, and we can underestimate how God might be working through them but when we ask in those moments, 'God, what are you doing through my child?' it can lead to a powerful encounter for ourselves or others.

Sometimes it can feel like everyone else knows what they're doing, or that their kids are connecting with God when yours isn't. Having worked with lots of parents I can assure you that we're all winging it and trying to figure out how to do faith as a family as we go along. That is part of the beauty. We're all on different journeys, finding our own rhythms.

I've mentioned it before but if you would like to be more equipped at sharing faith with your kids, I highly recommend the Parenting for Faith course (parentingforfaith.org). It's helped me to trust God more and find real joy in doing faith alongside my kids. As well as chatting to God and hearing from Him, it's given me a lot more confidence discussing faith topics with my kid. When he asks me, 'How can Jesus live in our hearts?' or 'What will our new bodies be like in heaven?' I don't feel pressured to give him big answers, I feel excited about asking him what *he* thinks and exploring the answers together.

When I read Bible stories with my kids when they were young, I always asked God to speak to me as well – both through the story and whatever they said about it. **Adrian**

. . . .

I think, as parents, we spend so much time feeling guilty about what we *aren't* doing that we don't see what we *are* doing. We choose a couple of songs each night from a worship song book to sing (mostly to save us from singing *Twinkle, Twinkle, Little Star* every night), and over time the kids have started learning some of them and can now choose. I had tears of joy running down my cheeks recently at bedtime as my young boys belted out *10,000 Reasons* at the top of their voices followed by *O Come, All Ye Faithful*. To know they have those words in their heads and hearts as they go about their days is so wonderful. We will never have all the answers but we have a wonderful Father that will use each seed we offer. **Diane**

. . . .

We have just started doing 'Favourites and Hardest' at the end of each day, where we each say what was our favourite bit of the day and what was the hardest. We then thank God for the favourites and for Him being *with us in the hardest. The goal is to encourage us all to think about what has been positive and what God does when we are struggling. My husband and I are finding it pretty helpful too!* **Katharine**

Doing faith as an individual, as a couple or as a family, will look different for each of us. There is no one right way to do it. You know your kids and God gave them to you. You get the privilege of being the person to show them what it means to 'Love the LORD your God with all your heart and with all your soul and with all your strength' (Deut. 6:5).

THINKING HONESTLY

How can you intentionally connect with God? Through listening to worship music, reading the Bible, listening to sermons or podcasts or simply by chatting to God throughout the day?

What do you need to do in order to connect with God at church? Could you ask someone else to hold your baby for a few minutes during sung worship? Could you join a midweek group?

[1]Louie Giglio and Matt Redman, *Indescribable* (Colorado Springs, CO, USA: David C. Cook, 2011)
[2]Hillsong Young & Free, *Heart of God*

Final thoughts

Parenthood can feel relentless, exhausting and lonely. But it can also feel awe-inspiring, joy-filled and incredibly fulfilling. No one else has parented *our* kids and the experience of parenthood is different for each one of us. However, there are many shared challenges. There are many opportunities for us to stand alongside each other, to encourage one another, to pray for one another and to be honest and vulnerable with each other.

Sharing my experiences of parenthood doesn't mean that I'm no longer dropping balls, or feeling completely shattered. I will probably never achieve everything I'd like to, and I will continue daily to make mistakes. But I am not powerless. I have choices. I can choose to be present. I can choose to hold each ball lightly or allow some to drop. I can choose to seek out community and connection, and to be open, honest and vulnerable. I can choose to talk about everything: the challenges *and* the moments of deep joy.

When we choose connection with God, our partners, our kids and our friends and family, our experience of parenthood may still sometimes be hard but it will no longer be lonely. Connection grows from honest and vulnerable conversations. It begins in those moments when we choose to share just a little bit more of ourselves than we would normally.

On the days when we tell our kids we love them and

they reply, 'You're a funny lady.' Or we say to them in desperation, 'I really just want to have a wee on my own,' and they go away only to reappear with a triangle and say, 'OK, I'll sing to you then.' We need those moments of connection with our community even more. We need the friends who say, 'I know exactly how you feel,' and mean it.

Whatever season of parenthood you are in, whether you are yet to have children or they have grown up and left home already, I pray that you would find more connection in the messiness of everyday life. I pray that God would give you boldness and confidence to share more of yourself than you normally would. I pray that you would find yourself part of a supportive community, which enables you to be loved and encouraged whatever parenthood looks like for you.

I pray that you will find joy in this season, through all the different challenges that parenthood brings. And that as you savour every small moment you spend in His presence, your relationship with Him will grow deeper than ever before.

Acknowledgements

Pete Willmot, for always believing in me, journeying alongside me and creating space for me to be creative and pursue my dreams.

Big brother and Little brother, for making me a mum. I adore you both, you make my heart so happy.

My mum, Heather Wyeth, for always supporting me, and inspiring me to be the mum that I am.

My family, Merv Wyeth, Ed and Emily Wyeth, and Fi Stevenson, for your constant encouragement and faith in me.

Rachel Turner, for believing in me and my book before I even knew I would write one.

Emma Pilcher, for that first honest conversation and the many since.

Hannah and Joe Widdows, Nick and Becky Drake, Jos and John Hudson, Dan and Mel Bright, Louisa Goodwin and Katharine Welby-Roberts, and my mums prayer group: I am so grateful for your friendship. This book wouldn't be what it is if it wasn't for you.

Thank you to my 'Forge Warrior Women' for your wisdom during my time as a kids pastor and into motherhood.

Thank you to all of my family, friends and church community who loved and supported me as I wrote this book, and contributed your knowledge and experiences into the conversation.

Journey through family life together...

Take time out each day to encounter the God who created you, loves you and has plans for each of you! Over 12 weeks discover more about what it means to follow God, as Steve and Bekah Legg bring a fun, engaging and personal approach to reading the Bible.

> **❝** A great resource to bring the family together to talk about the things that matter. **❞**
> **Rob Parsons**

ISBN:978-1-78951-264-9   ISBN:978-1-78259-999-9   ISBN: 978-1-78259-798-8   ISBN: 978-1-78259-692-9

Bekah is the director of mission at Maybridge Community Church, and Steve is the founding editor of *Sorted* magazine. They are experienced parents of five daughters.

To find out more and to order, visit **cwr.org.uk/thefamilydevotional** or call **01252 784700**.

Also available in Christian bookshops.